WAYS OF INVESTING IN CRYPTOCURRENCY

The Smart Investor's Guide to Making Money in Crypto

…. Yonas Gebremichael

About the Author

Yonas Gebremichael is a multifaceted professional who combines his passion for Information Technology with his expertise *in Artificial Intelligence, Blockchain Technology* and *Cryptocurrency Investments*. He has authored several books and blogs on these topics, sharing his insights and knowledge with a wide audience.

As a cryptocurrency entrepreneur, he has founded two innovative companies: one is a start-up that offers a cryptocurrency exchange platform, and the *other (Digital Habesha Cryptocurrency Entrepreneurship - **DHCE**)* is a company that provides various services related to crypto, such as brokerage, trading strategy, market analysis, Blockchain technology, Metaverse, DeFi, NFT, and more.

In addition to this one, he has written two books specifically about crypto: *Master Cryptocurrency Trading, and Bitcoin Trading and Hacking*. These books cover the essential aspects of crypto trading and security, from the basics to the advanced techniques.

Contact and Follow the Author on social media:

Email: bitcoindigger2020@gmail.com
Instagram: instagram.com/cyber_rapper
Facebook: Yonas Gebremichael
Telegram discussion group: https://t.me/digital_habeshachat

Before you read

You might wonder why you should invest in cryptocurrency when you have other FinTech or traditional investment methods available. Well, smart people keep up with the latest technology and the most convenient options. Here are the reasons why cryptocurrencies are a good investment idea:

- Cryptocurrencies offer privacy, cost-effectiveness, and decentralization, which may appeal to some investors who value these features.
- Cryptocurrencies have high liquidity and potential for high returns, as they can be easily traded and have shown rapid growth in the past.
- Cryptocurrencies can diversify your portfolio and give you more choices, as there are many different coins to choose from and they may have low correlation with other assets.
- Cryptocurrencies may be the future of money and technology, as they have the potential to revolutionize various industries and provide a secure and transparent way of transactions.
- Crypto allows users to send money beyond borders at low costs and quick processing times.
- Cryptocurrencies are traded 24 hours a day, 7 days a week, unlike traditional investments and foreign exchange markets, which are closed on weekends…etc.

Introduction

Thank you for downloading the book, **"Ways of investing in cryptocurrency!"**

This book will teach you the essential concepts of cryptocurrency from the beginning. By the time you finish reading this guide, you will be more knowledgeable about cryptocurrencies than most people you know. You will also be prepared to take on the role of an early adopter, identifying the right new currencies to get involved with at the right time and in the right way. Most people think that cryptocurrency investment only involves trading and holding. However, there are dozens of ways to earn cryptocurrency passively or without much effort. In this book, you will find convenient alternative investments that can change your life.

In the first part, the introductory section on **Cryptocurrency 101**, you will learn what cryptocurrency is, the different cryptocurrencies, network fees, crypto wallets, and more. Then, under **Blockchain 101**, you will learn the basics of blockchain and how it works. The real practical guide starts in part two, where this book focuses more. Here you will learn about the different ways to invest in cryptocurrency, with detailed information on each topic. This part provides a comprehensive guide on how to invest in cryptocurrency profitably by choosing an investment option that suits you. I have covered every point, so all you have to do is read attentively.

Table of Contents

Part One:

Introduction to Cryptocurrency and Blockchain

Cryptocurrency 101

What is cryptocurrency?

Cryptocurrency, often called "crypto," is any type of **decentralized, digital currency that's based on cryptography**. Those three terms are key to understanding the thousands of types of crypto being traded today.

Decentralized means that cryptocurrency isn't issued by a central authority like a government or bank, the way the dollar, euro, yen, and other fiat currencies are. Instead, cryptocurrencies are created, exchanged, and overseen by a distributed peer-to-peer network.

Crypto is digital, meaning two things. First, with a couple of exceptions, the value of most crypto is not pegged to a fiat currency like the dollar or euro, nor is it determined by a precious metal like gold. And though people may refer to crypto in physical terms (e.g., as coins), crypto is generated and traded in only a digital format.

Cryptography refers to the mathematical technique used to secure each unit of cryptocurrency and ensure it can't be copied.

Most crypto exists on a blockchain platform. Blockchain is the **digital ledger** that records most crypto transactions. This use of blockchain technology as a foundational element for cryptocurrency began in 2009, in tandem with the launch of Bitcoin. But blockchain technology is evolving rapidly, and a range of other industries are exploring its potential applications as well. We will see what is blockchain, its use cases and everything about it in details later.

How does cryptocurrency work?

Today there are thousands of cryptocurrencies, and while many are designed to provide some new feature or function on a given blockchain platform, most are founded on similar principles to those that established Bitcoin. Crypto is secured by a **peer-to-peer network**, and users can trade or transfer value — globally and almost instantly, 24/7 — without relying on a middleman like a bank or payment processor.

Cryptocurrencies are considered secure because they employ a "trustless" system of verification for all transactions. This means that users don't have to rely on a third party to verify transactions: the system itself is self-governing.

As of the year 2021, estimates of the number of cryptocurrencies you could trade ranged from about 6,000 coins to over 10,000, with a total market capitalization of over $2 trillion. And now as of 2023, the number is increased surprisingly to more than 12,000, the biggest cryptocurrencies by market capitalization are Bitcoin, Ethereum, Binance Coin, Tether and Solana. Cryptocurrencies are generally stored in digital wallets, commonly a blockchain wallet, which allows users to manage and trade different crypto.

How does crypto mining work?

Crypto miners use special computer hardware to do the complex mathematical cryptography required to confirm each transaction on a blockchain. This process, called **"proof of work" (PoW)**, requires miners to complete billions of calculations in order to verify a block of transactions. **Proof of stake (PoS)** is another consensus mechanism by which crypto is created, but PoW is common to many forms of crypto.

Crypto mining is highly competitive. The process relies on a network-wide consensus that essentially backs the validity of each transaction, even without a central authority. Once a miner has completed a certain number of calculations to verify a block of transactions on a given blockchain platform, they may be rewarded with new coins — if they are the first to verify the block.

Because proof-of-work crypto mining requires immense amounts of energy, there are concerns that the types of crypto that rely on PoW may be harmful to the environment.

What are crypto exchanges?

With the exception of emerging crypto-based securities, it's generally not possible to trade crypto on a traditional exchange, which is why you need a crypto exchange.

There are three main types of crypto exchanges: centralized, decentralized, and hybrid. While centralized exchanges are still more common for trading crypto, it's important to understand the differences among the three so you can decide which is best for you.

Centralized

A centralized cryptocurrency exchange is a platform where cryptos are bought and sold, with the help of a third party to conduct these transactions. On a centralized exchange you can use a traditional, a.k.a. fiat currency, like the dollar to execute trades, as well as trading crypto itself.

Decentralized

Decentralized exchanges (DEX) are more aligned with the spirit of crypto, in that these exchanges allow crypto investors to trade directly with each other, without the need for a middleman. In theory, a DEX might be more secure since there's no central platform that can be hacked. Also, without the need for third parties, you might see lower fees and faster transaction speeds on a DEX.

Hybrid

Hybrid exchanges are less common than either centralized or decentralized exchanges. They aim to combine features of both: e.g., the liquidity of a centralized exchange and the security and anonymity of a DEX.

When choosing the exchange where you prefer to trade crypto, there are other issues to consider, including ease of use, whether your funds might be insured, as well as other considerations.

Bitcoin and Beyond

Bitcoin: The OG Crypto

Bitcoin (BTC) was the first cryptocurrency to be created in 2009 by a person (or possibly a group) using the pseudonym **Satoshi Nakamoto**. Bitcoin was designed to be independent of any government or central bank. Instead, it relies on blockchain technology, a decentralized public ledger that contains a digital record of every bitcoin transaction.

In essence, Bitcoin established the basic system of cryptography and consensus (i.e., peer-to-peer) verification that is the foundation of most forms of crypto today.

How Bitcoin Works

Bitcoin miners use powerful computers to verify blocks of transactions and generate more bitcoins — a complex, time-consuming process called **proof-of-work (PoW).** Each block of transactions is logged permanently on the blockchain, which helps to validate and secure each bitcoin and the network as a whole. Owing to the vast number of computers or nodes on the bitcoin blockchain, the PoW process ends up using so much energy that many people question whether it's sustainable.

How To Get Bitcoin /or altcoins?

There are a few different ways to buy bitcoin.

- **Exchanges**. As noted above, you can trade crypto — including bitcoin — on centralized, decentralized, or hybrid exchanges. All you need is a crypto wallet for storing your bitcoins.
- **ATMs**. There are several thousand crypto ATMs where you can purchase bitcoin: estimates range from 14,000 to 26,000. Unlike a traditional ATM, though, you can't withdraw actual cash from these machines; they make digital only transactions via the blockchain.
- **Brokerages**. A growing number of brokers now allow you to buy and sell crypto, similar to any other security, for example Binance and Kucoin.

Pros and Cons of Bitcoin

Bitcoin may be the oldest and most popular form of crypto (by market share), but it comes with its pros and cons.

Market capitalization. The crypto-verse has thousands of players, but bitcoin outstrips them all, with a market cap of over $502 billion as of Sep 2023. For context: Ethereum, the number 2 crypto by market cap, is about half that is at $200 billion.

Volatility. In 2021 alone, the value of bitcoin ranged from about $29,000 on January 1 to $64,000 in mid-April, dropping to about $26,600 in late July and rising to about $64,000 again as of Nov. 15. Even within the course of a single day, the value can fluctuate by thousands.

Not SIPC insured. Most investors are insured by the SIPC up to $500,000 if a brokerage fails (or funds are stolen). But the SIPC doesn't cover crypto.

Regulation and usage. The inconsistency of regulations governing crypto has limited the use of these currencies around the world. But a number of companies accept bitcoin as means of payment.

Meet the altcoins: Bitcoin alternatives

"Altcoin" is a catch-all term for alternative cryptocurrencies to bitcoin.

There are many different altcoins — different types, and within those categories, different specific products. Litecoin is generally recognized as the first altcoin.

Ethereum (ETH)

Unlike Bitcoin, Ethereum wasn't created to support a currency — but as a programmable blockchain, to enable the network's users to create, **publish**, **monetize**, and use **applications (called dApps).** Ether (ETH) was developed as a form of payment on the Ethereum platform. ETH was also generated using a proof-of-work system (note that Ethereum moved to PoS now). But unlike Bitcoin, there is no limit to the number of ETHs that can be created. Ethereum has helped fuel many initial coin offerings (ICOs), and the Ethereum blockchain has also been behind the boom in **non-fungible tokens** (NFTs).

Litecoin (LTC)

Litecoin was created from a fork in the bitcoin blockchain, and it was designed to enable almost instant, near-zero cost payments that can be exchanged between people or institutions worldwide. Litecoin uses a proof-of-work system (PoW) to verify transactions on the blockchain, but owing to certain modifications it's considered a "lighter," faster version of Bitcoin. The main difference between Litecoin and Bitcoin is that Litecoin uses a mining algorithm called scrypt to enable faster transaction times.

Cardano (ADA)

Cardano (ADA) was launched in 2017 by the co-founder of Ethereum, and has positioned itself as a next-level player. Cardano relies on proof-of-stake (PoS), rather than the complicated PoW calculations required for Bitcoin and others, potentially making its network more efficient and sustainable. Cardano is being built in five phases toward achieving its goal of developing the network into a decentralized application (dApp) platform with a multi-asset ledger and verifiable smart contracts. Cardano's cryptocurrency is called ADA, after Ada Lovelace, a 19th-century mathematician.

Polkadot (DOT)

Polkadot was co-founded by Gavin Wood, also a co-founder of Ethereum, to take the capabilities of a blockchain network to another level. The blockchain's cryptocurrency is called dot.

Polkadot operates using two blockchains — the main "relay" network, where transactions are permanent, and a parallel network of user-created blockchains, called "**parachains**." Parachains can be customized for myriad uses like building apps (they can even support other coins). What differentiates Polkadot from other blockchains is its core mission to solve the problem of interoperability (the ability of blockchains to communicate with other blockchains) by building so-called **bridges** between blockchains.

Bitcoin Cash (BCH)

Bitcoin Cash was created in 2017, after some developers became frustrated with the slowdown of Bitcoin transactions (and subsequent higher fees) as Bitcoin's 1MB (2k tx) data blocks filled up. So they executed a hard fork on the Bitcoin blockchain and came up with Bitcoin Cash, which has a much larger block size of 8MB. For users, that means faster processing speeds and lower fees. You will learn what fork is later on.

Dogecoin (DOGE)

Dogecoin (pronounced dohj-coin) is widely known as the first joke cryptocurrency or meme coin; it was launched in 2013 as an altcoin and it runs on a blockchain network using a PoW system similar to Bitcoin and

Ethereum. But the number of coins that can be mined are unlimited (versus the 21 million-coin cap on Bitcoin). Despite its place as one of the biggest coins by market cap, Dogecoin trades at one of the lowest prices as of the writing of this book.

Understanding Defi Tokens

DeFi, short for decentralized finance, is disrupting legacy financial models by providing the same financial services (e.g., lending, trading, payments, etc.) using blockchain technology, thus theoretically making financial products and services more affordable and accessible. DeFi encompasses many new products: e.g. dApps (or dapps), which are decentralized computer programs built primarily on the Ethereum blockchain and governed by smart contracts, as well as crypto coins and tokens.

What is the difference between DeFi coins and tokens?

DeFi coins (like Bitcoin) are similar to fiat coins in that they are fungible, and they're a digital means of storing and transferring value.
The important thing to know about **DeFi tokens** is they are more like financial tools, meaning that tokens are non-fungible assets, and perform other functions than just being a store of value. Many DeFi tokens offer innovative solutions to existing blockchain problems, and for this reason may provide different opportunities for investors than being a store of value. Following are a few common DeFi tokens.

Tezos (XTZ)

Like other platforms, Tezos utilizes blockchain to produce a decentralized computing platform: Users verify the code and data on the blockchain, and through that process, receive XTZ or tez tokens. The tez isn't mined but rather relies on a unique, "liquid" proof-of-stake (PoS) model. Although some blockchains empower developers and miners to make choices about the platform, Tezos has developed an on-chain governance model that allows changes to the platform's protocol when the community approves proposals to upgrade. This helps Tezos to avoid hard forks, which can be disruptive to the entire blockchain.

Uniswap (UNI)

Uniswap is an open-source software protocol built on the Ethereum blockchain that allows investors to trade cryptocurrency directly with one another without intermediaries. And because it's open source, virtually anyone can create a decentralized exchange using their code. The Uniswap exchange (a typical example of Decentralised exchange) has also garnered attention because of the **UNI** token, a governance token, as well as its use of automated liquidity pools.

Chainlink (LINK)

The Chainlink network is a decentralized "oracle" network built on the Ethereum blockchain to facilitate the transfer of data from off-chain sources to on-chain smart contracts — in effect, becoming a bridge between external data sources and smart contracts. Every oracle (or data provider) on the network is incentivized by being assigned a reputation score based on the accuracy of the data they provide, and may be further rewarded with Chainlink's currency.

SushiSwap (SUSHI)

SushiSwap was created from a hard fork off the prominent DeFi exchange, Uniswap, in 2020. It's considered an **automated market maker (AMM)** that enables users to trade different types of crypto assets. But it's a decentralized exchange, so there's no central authority monitoring trades. Traders on SushiSwap use liquidity pools to trade, and trades are processed using smart contracts.

Wrapped Bitcoin (WBTC)

Wrapped bitcoin is the ERC-20 token that represents one bitcoin and can be used in decentralized applications (DApps). With WBTC, users essentially can use Bitcoin in the Ethereum ecosystem where they otherwise wouldn't be able to. DApps can process wrapped token transactions faster because there is no need for computation to happen across different blockchains, which is a difficult process. Thus, WBTC helps to bring the liquidity of Bitcoin to the Ethereum network, allowing people to combine the price value of Bitcoin with the programmability of Ethereum.

The Graph (GRT)

The Graph Network and its token, GRT, are relatively new. GRT is an Ethereum-based token that powers the Graph, which is a decentralized query protocol built for querying and indexing data from different blockchains. The Graph also allows users to build APIs, known as subgraphs, to allow applications to talk to each other, and it also makes querying networks fast and secure. GRT is its native token.

Non-Fungible Tokens (NFTs)

Non-Fungible Tokens, NFTs, are cryptographic digital assets that have uniquely identifiable metadata and codes. An NFT's data is stored on a blockchain like Ethereum (which supports many NFTs) or up-and-comers like Tezos, ensuring that the NFT can't be replicated or forged.
The tokens act as a representation for either digital or tangible items — like digital artwork, virtual real estate in a game, collectible Pokemon cards, or a tokenized version of the first-ever tweet, created by Twitter CEO Jack Dorsey (which sold for $2.9 million in March 2021).
The real value of NFTs is still emerging, but already these tokens are transforming art, travel, gaming, even supply chains and personal identification, thanks to the use of blockchain technology, which is designed to prevent duplication and fraud and takes issues like ownership and personal data security to a new level.

What are Crypto Networks?

The crypto community seem to love synonyms. You may hear terms like the Bitcoin blockchain, the Bitcoin network, and the Bitcoin protocol; these essentially refer to the same thing: the blockchain network that the Bitcoin protocol runs on.

The same goes for other networks/protocols/blockchains like Ethereum, Binance Smart Chain, Cardano, Avalanche, Algorand, Solana etc. So there are dozens of different networks and tens of thousands of different tokens running on all these networks.

What on Earth am I talking about with all these networks? Isn't it all just crypto?

To be blunt, no. This is where things can get confusing. If you have only ever held and traded crypto on a centralized exchange such as Binance or Kucoin, then crypto may seem straightforward.

But, in reality, there are base layer protocols, payment protocols, privacy coins, smart contract networks, scaling networks, oracles, interoperability projects, DAGs, DAOs, stablecoins, lending tokens, tokens for content monetization, file storage projects, mesh networking, energy projects, video streaming projects, and seriously countless other projects and protocols that are often entirely different. It's enough to make one's head spin!

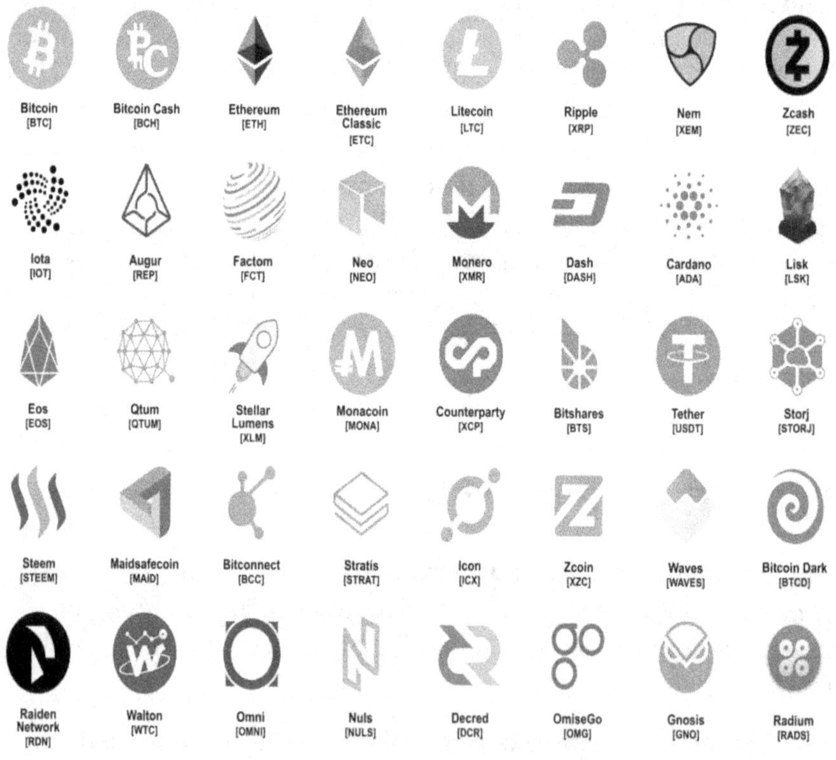

Just a Sample of the Hundreds of Thousands of Tokens in Existence: Image via Shutterstock

Users can swap and trade completely different assets from different protocols/networks like Bitcoin for Ethereum with no problem on centralised exchanges. This is really convenient as users can shuffle crypto assets around like a pack of cards and not think about what is happening on the underlying networks.

When exchanging crypto on an exchange, you are not magically turning your Bitcoin into Ethereum; that isn't possible. What is actually happening behind the scenes is that the Bitcoin is being sold, and the funds are being used to buy Ethereum.

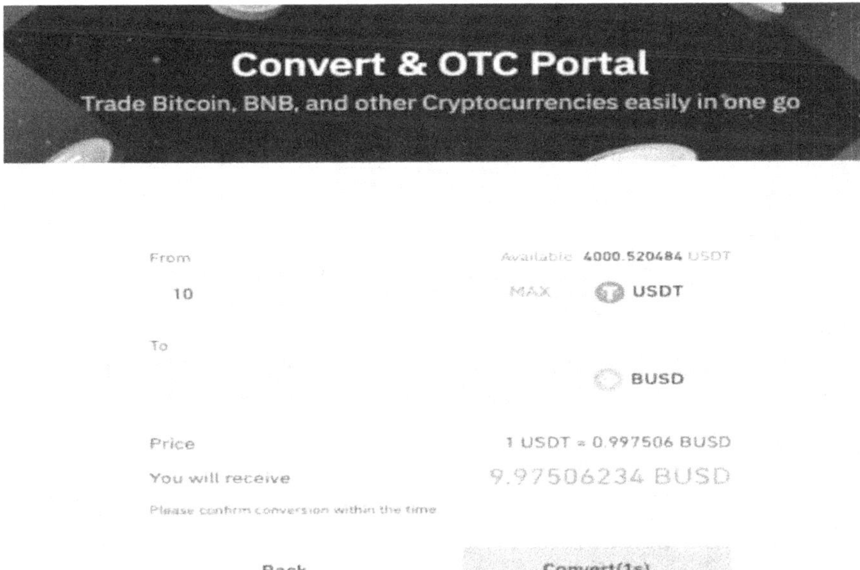

Swapping Crypto on Exchanges Looks Simple on the Surface, Image via Binance

The buying and selling of these assets will incur network fees that the exchange takes care of behind the scenes. The user is simply being charged a transaction fee by the exchange company. **Transaction fees** and **network fees** are different. While the terminology may change slightly depending on the exchange or platform and is sometimes used interchangeably, typically, transaction fees go to the exchange or platform. Network fees go to the underlying network and are paid to the network miners and validators. More on them later.

Users may not always see a network fee on a centralized exchange, but these will become important when moving crypto off of an exchange when looking to **self-custody**, getting involved with Decentralized exchanges like Uniswap or other DeFi platforms, mint NFTs etc.

When I said that it was impossible to swap and turn Bitcoin into Ethereum, allow me to explain what I mean.

Each native cryptocurrency can only run and exist solely on its own network, and each cryptocurrency protocol is different. Bitcoin runs on the Bitcoin network, Ethereum runs on the Ethereum network, Solana runs on the Solana network, etc.

There are things like **cross-chain bridges**, **wrapped tokens**, **wormholes**, and projects like ThorChain, Cosmos, and Polkadot that provide cross-chain capabilities, but for the simplicity of this article, let's take it back to basics. I use Bitcoin and Ethereum as an example, but these same principles apply to any crypto-asset that runs on different networks.

Cryptocurrency networks do not play well with each other. Assets like Bitcoin and Ethereum are like trains running on their own tracks. Just as a train cannot hop off its track and onto another track, neither can cryptocurrencies. Each crypto network is essentially its own track and does not cross with other network tracks, so Bitcoin never leaves the Bitcoin network, Ethereum never leaves the Ethereum network, and neither Bitcoin nor Ethereum can run on other networks unless it is a "wrapped" version of the asset.

I find it helps to visualize this. The Bitcoin network is only home to Bitcoin like this:

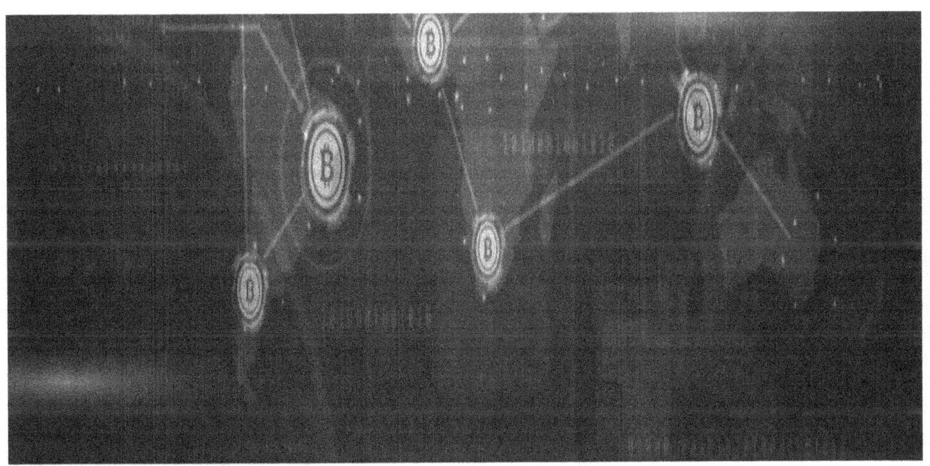

The Ethereum network is only home to Ethereum and Ethereum based ERC20 tokens like this:

Cryptocurrency networks do not work like this:

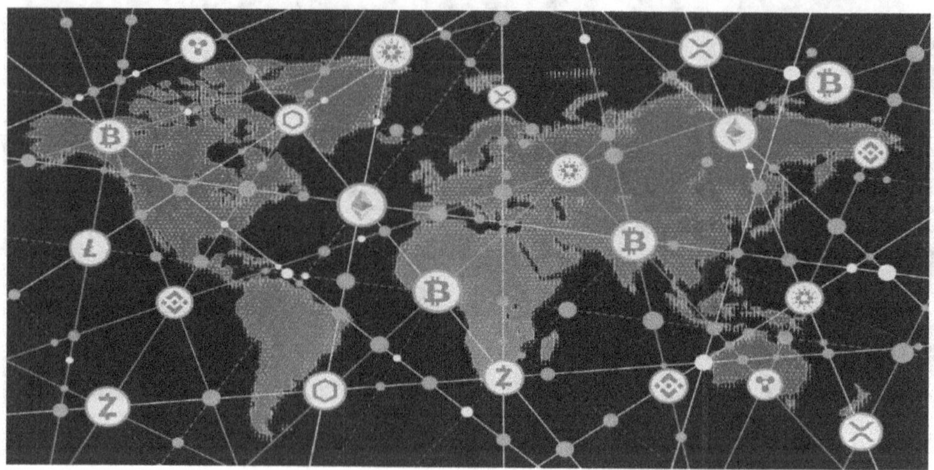

The image above makes it look like crypto tokens are **interchangeable** and **interoperable**, all flowing seamlessly on the same network, which is not the case. However, this is the eventual goal that projects like **Polkadot** and **Cosmos** are trying to achieve, as this is the interoperable crypto future, we all dream of, and it would be great if all crypto networks were someday linked but we are likely many years away from that.

If you never plan to send your funds off of the exchange where you bought them, you do not really need to worry about this stuff. But if you ever decide that you want to self-custody your crypto, send it to other exchanges, wallets, platforms, or get involved in the wonderful world of <u>DeFi</u>, then you are going to want to pay attention and make sure you don't send a token on the wrong network, as that could result in a permanent loss of funds in some cases.

Network Fees

As mentioned, sometimes the exchange or platform will cover the network fee, but anytime you are sending crypto from a wallet, DeFi protocol/exchange, or anytime when there is no centralized authority involved, you will likely encounter a network fee, also sometimes called a transaction fee just to confuse everyone.

Here's what I mean, two very popular self-custodial wallets are the **MetaMask** wallet and the **Exodus** wallet. One refers to the Ethereum fee as a network fee. The other is a transaction fee (Metamask). I mentioned how the crypto community loves synonyms, which is also often called a **Gas fee**. I will be explaining gas fees later on.

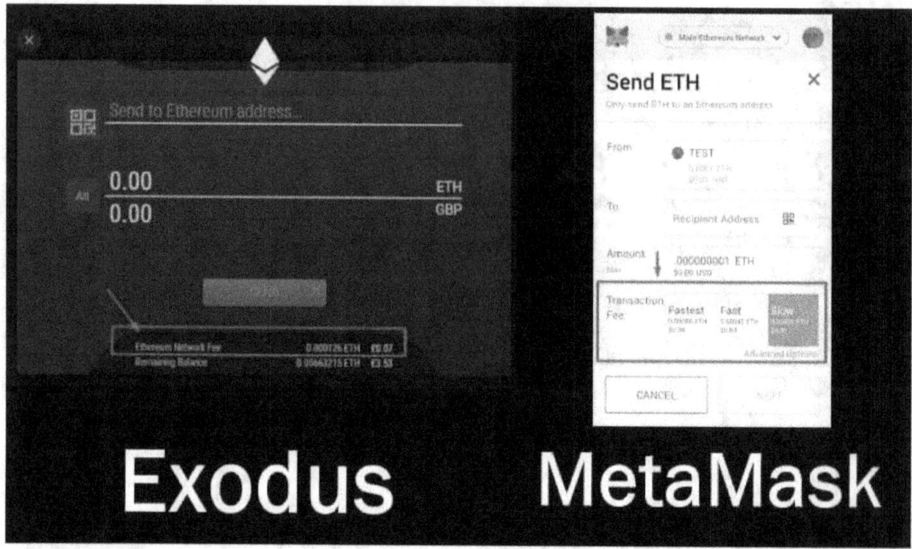

The network fees you will need to pay will vary depending on the network. For example, when someone wants to send Bitcoin, the network fee is paid in Bitcoin. When someone wants to send Ethereum, the fee gets paid in Ethereum. Solana is paid in Solana, and so on, which makes sense. You can think of a blockchain's native asset as similar to fuel, aka gas, as it is called for Ethereum. It's that gas/fuel needed to power transactions for any token that runs on that network.

Where it can get confusing is that there are tens of thousands of tokens built on some networks that use the same metaphorical railway. Ethereum is the largest and most complex ecosystem, and example of this. Tokens such as Chainlink (LINK), Decentraland (MANA), The Sandbox (SAND), Uniswap (UNI), stablecoins like USDT and USDC and thousands of others also run on the Ethereum network, so **ERC20 tokens** (AKA Ethereum based tokens) do not have their own network, they run on the Ethereum network. Because of that, users need to pay network fees in Ethereum, as Ethereum is the "fuel/gas" needed to send any one of the thousands of Ethereum based assets.

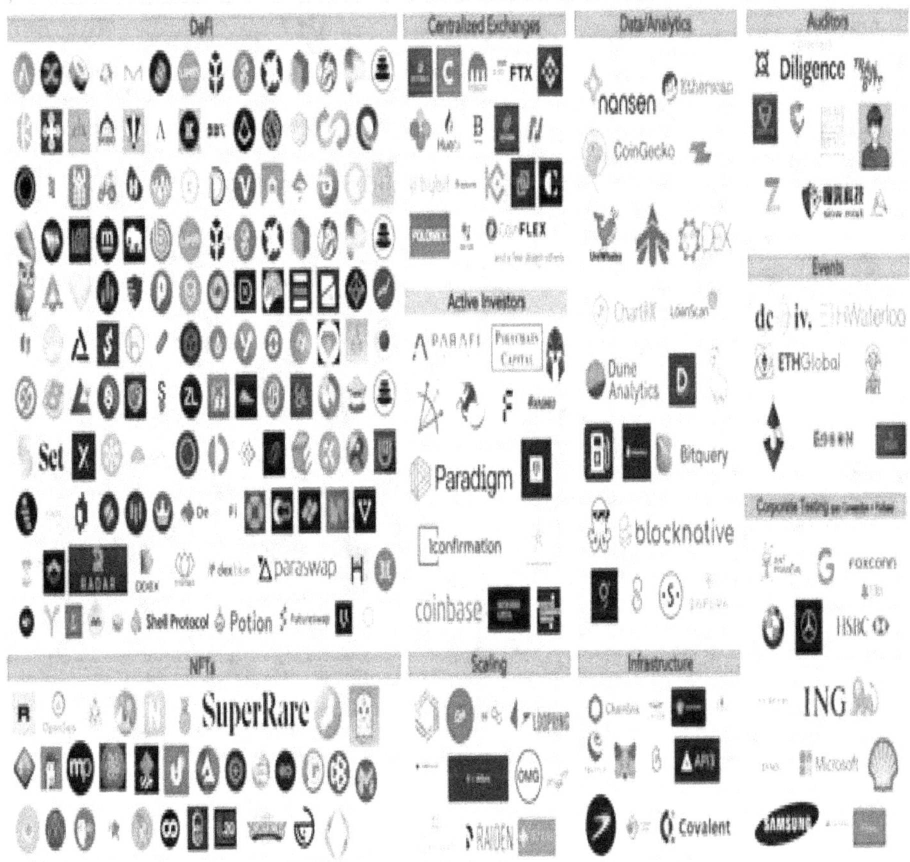

Diagram Showing Only a Small Fraction of the Ethereum Ecosystem- It's Massive!

Chainlink was one of the first crypto assets I ever purchased. However, the first time I tried to send it to a wallet, I was hit with an error message saying, "You don't have enough Ethereum!" which I found confusing as I was trying to send Chainlink, not Ethereum? I didn't understand why I needed ETH, so I was met with a message very similar to the one below:

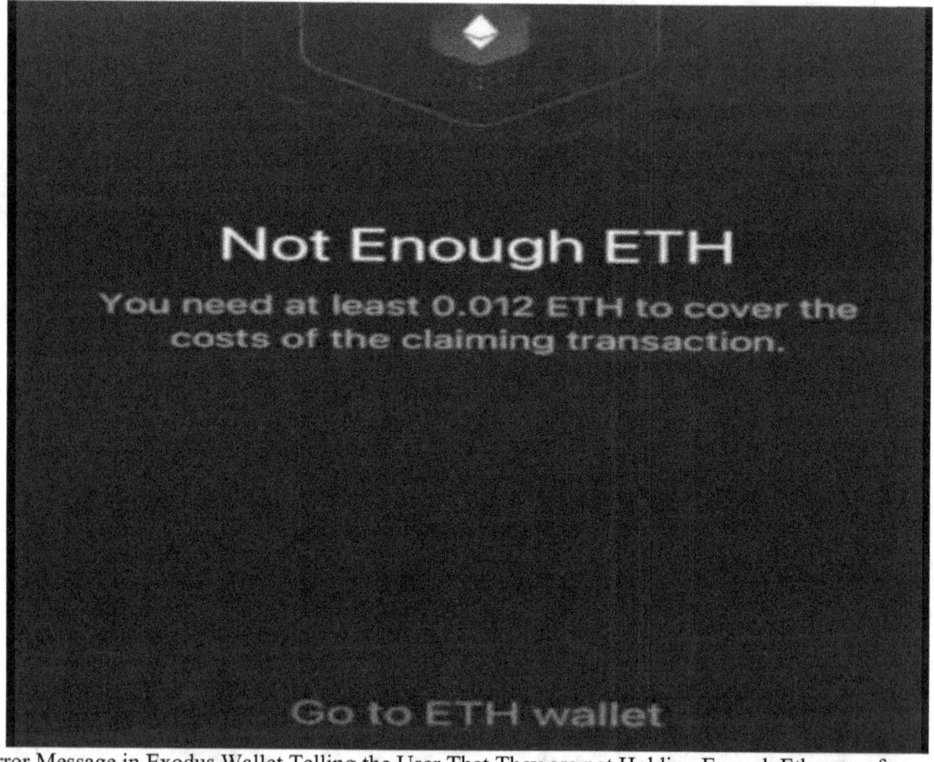

Error Message in Exodus Wallet Telling the User That They are not Holding Enough Ethereum for an Ethereum based token transaction.

I remember the crazy amount of outrage that existed during the 2021 bull run from many new users to the crypto industry who didn't understand Ethereum gas fees.

People were writing scathingly negative reviews about crypto wallet companies all over the internet as the Ethereum gas fees were skyrocketing to hundreds of dollars, and people were mistakenly thinking

that the wallet companies and crypto platforms were charging these fees. There were threats of lawsuits; it was chaos. People did not understand that these fees had nothing to do with the crypto wallet company or decentralized platform; these fees were sent entirely to the Ethereum network miners who were dealing with record levels of traffic on the Eth network.

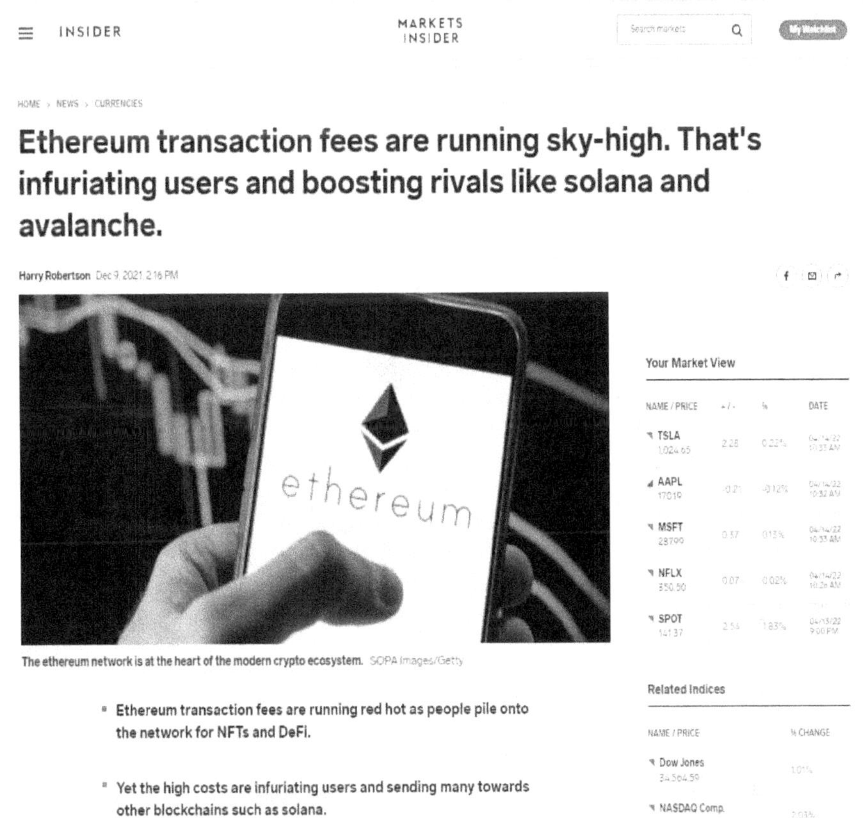

The ethereum network is at the heart of the modern crypto ecosystem. SOPA Images/Getty

- Ethereum transaction fees are running red hot as people pile onto the network for NFTs and DeFi.

- Yet the high costs are infuriating users and sending many towards other blockchains such as solana.

- Developers are scrambling to fix the problem, which could threaten ethereum's top-dog status.

Now, of course, I know, and so do you, that you need to hold Ethereum for gas to pay the network fees for any Ethereum based ERC20 token.

The same goes for the Solana network, BSC, Cardano etc. Whenever a network has a native token, the native token needs to be held as fuel to cover the network fees. So next time you go to send an asset like **PancakeSwap** (CAKE), you will know that the fee needs to be paid in BNB token, or any Polygon tokens need to be fueled by holding the MATIC token etc. These network fees are paid automatically, so you need to make sure you are holding some of the native tokens in your wallet, and you are good to go.

There are a few exceptions to this rule. Some crypto ecosystems run a two token type system where one token is used to cover fees on the network. The prominent examples of this are **VeChain** which has fees that need to be paid in VeThor. Theta, which has fees that need to be paid in Theta Fuel. Neo, which has fees that need to be paid in Gas. And Ontology has fees that need to be paid in Ontology Gas.

The Two Token System for Vechain and VeThor

Why are there Network Fees?

We know fees can be a royal pain and nobody likes paying them, but nobody wants to work for free. Fees are how we pay for convenient services to be provided that make our lives better. We pay fees to enjoy Netflix, fees to enjoy Spotify, fees for food and shelter etc., and we pay fees to use Cryptocurrency as well.

Nearly every transaction recorded on the blockchain will incur a network fee. It doesn't matter if you are using the Ethereum network, Bitcoin network, Ripple, Cardano, Solana, Polkadot, or one of the other networks.

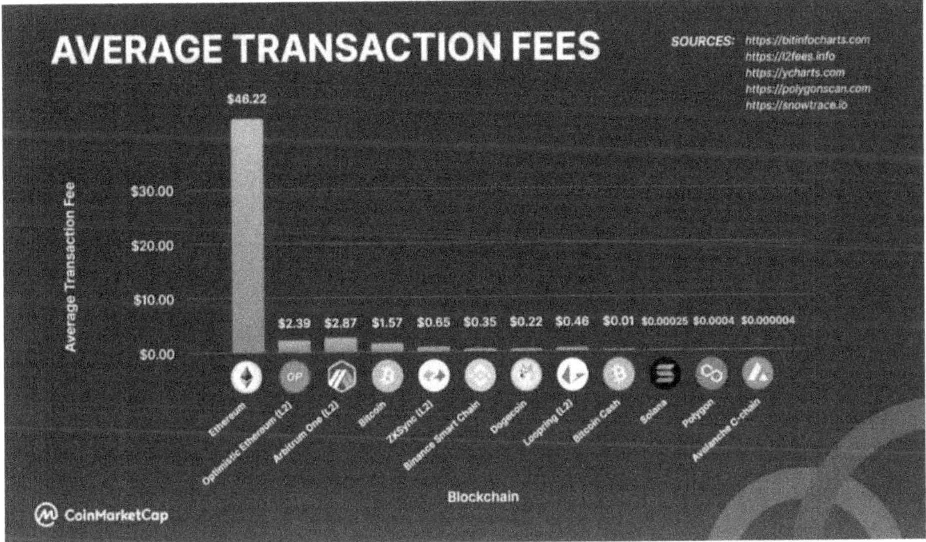

Comparing Some of the Various Blockchain Fees

A couple of blockchain networks allow fee-free transactions that will be covered later on, but for the most part, just expect that network/gas fees will be part of life in the crypto world. But, hey, I'd rather pay crypto fees than bank fees any day!

Crypto fees aren't always a bad thing as someone needs to pay for the work being done by the network miners and validators who run the machines, nodes, and protocols that validate and confirm transactions and secure the network.

Fees go to Paying Bitcoin Miners to run Mining Farms like This.

Miners and Validators are the unsung heroes, the workhorses that support the blockchain infrastructure, and I don't mind paying them for their work. If it weren't for them, crypto couldn't be used!

Where do the Fees go?

When you send a crypto asset to a wallet or an exchange, for Proof-of-Work-based assets like Bitcoin, the transactions need to go through a network/blockchain/Bitcoin miner.

I'll skip the technical jargon to avoid boring you. Miners are basically computers dedicated to the network that solve complex algorithms to validate all transactions and prohibit fraudulent transactions or double-spend attacks.

When someone sends Bitcoin, they create a cryptographically secure transaction broadcasted through the internet on the Bitcoin network, which is picked up by the network of Bitcoin miners. The miners collect as many transactions as can fit into a block. Then their computers go to work, going through a mathematical process to verify the block and add it to the chain of past blocks, hence the "blockchain." Here is how that looks:

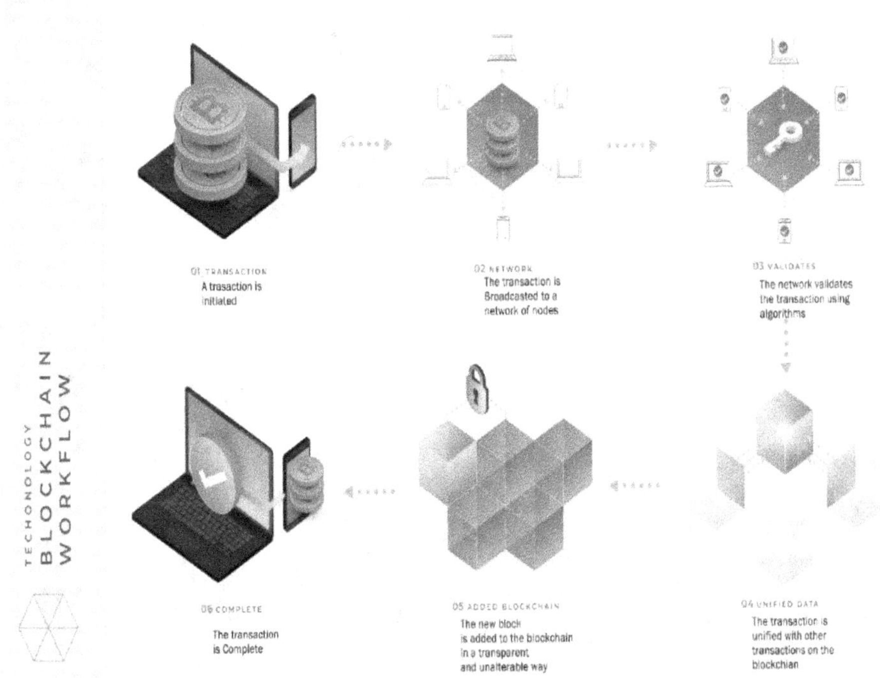

Miners get rewarded via freshly minted tokens for contributing their computing resources to the network. There is a lot of computing power needed to process crypto transactions. The resources to do so can be quite costly, so the network fee for crypto transactions goes to the folks who run these computers so we can send our beloved Proof-of-Work cryptocurrencies.

This process varies a lot depending on whether the token uses a Proof-of-Work, Proof-of-Stake, or one of the other consensus mechanisms. Proof of Work and Proof of Stake are very popular and Ethereum already moved to Proof-of-Stake. Some cryptocurrencies that use Proof-of-Stake or a variation are Cardano, Solana, Tezos, Avalanche, Algorand, and many others.

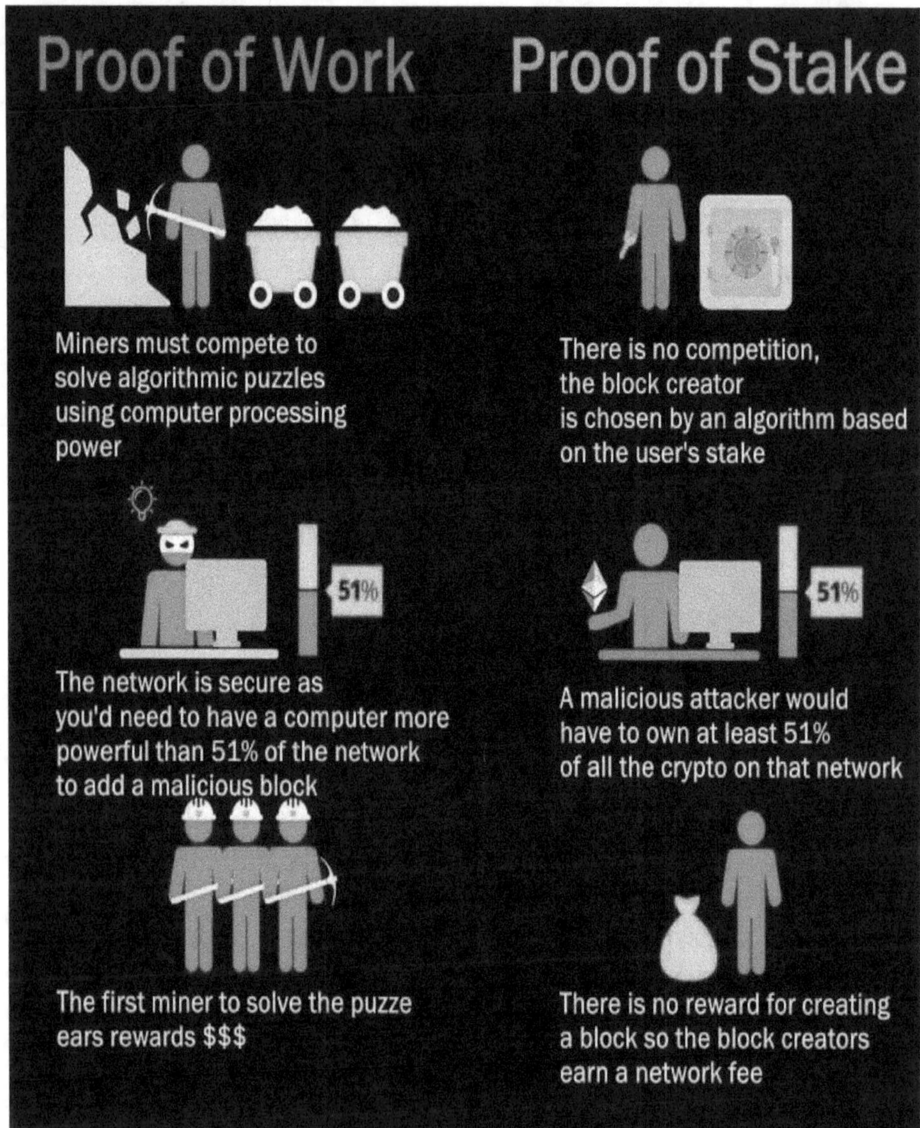

Cryptocurrencies allow owners of a crypto asset to stake coins and create their own validator nodes. Staking is the process of pledging your coins to be used to verify transactions. When someone stakes their crypto, those funds are locked up for the duration of the staking process, which varies depending on the asset.

When a block of transactions is ready to be processed, the Proof-of-Stake protocol will choose a validator node to review the block. The validator checks if the transactions are accurate, and if they are, that block gets added to the blockchain and the validator node that validated and processed the transaction receives rewards for its contribution. Those rewards are made up by the network fees that go along with transactions. Proof-of-Stake transactions require much less computational power, so therefore the transaction fees are generally substantially lower. Here is a look at how some of the different consensus mechanisms compare:

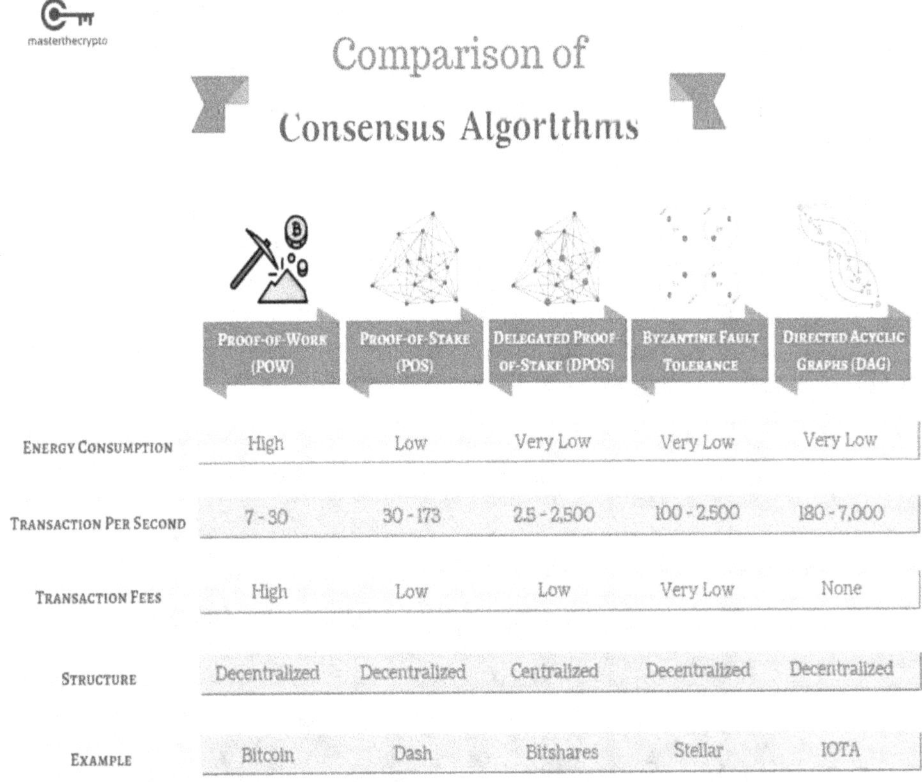

	PROOF-OF-WORK (POW)	PROOF-OF-STAKE (POS)	DELEGATED PROOF-OF-STAKE (DPOS)	BYZANTINE FAULT TOLERANCE	DIRECTED ACYCLIC GRAPHS (DAG)
ENERGY CONSUMPTION	High	Low	Very Low	Very Low	Very Low
TRANSACTION PER SECOND	7 - 30	30 - 173	2.5 - 2,500	100 - 2,500	180 - 7,000
TRANSACTION FEES	High	Low	Low	Very Low	None
STRUCTURE	Decentralized	Decentralized	Centralized	Decentralized	Decentralized
EXAMPLE	Bitcoin	Dash	Bitshares	Stellar	IOTA

Chart Comparing the Differences in Energy Consumption and Fees Between the Different Consensus Mechanisms

Solana, Algorand, and Avalanche simple transactions can be sent for fractions of a cent when network activity is low, making these among the cheapest PoS crypto networks. However, complex transactions on Avalanche have been reported as creeping above $10.

Networks With the Lowest, or No Fees.

We have talked a lot about what affects the fees for Proof-of-Work and Proof-of-Stake cryptos and discussed some Bitcoin and Ethereum alternatives with lower fees, but for the truly die-hard fee haters, there are even cheaper networks that will allow users to send crypto for free, or with fees so low they are practically negligible!

These cryptocurrencies are important as they are more useful as actual currency. For example, I don't mind paying 3 dollars for a Bitcoin network fee if I plan on only sending it once and holding it for a year, but I don't want to pay 3 dollars in fees for daily purchases and every time I go to the shop to buy candy (Haribo for the win!)

Allow me to introduce Ripple (XRP) and Stellar (XLM) tokens. While Ripple and Stellar both run on their own networks, these networks are neither Proof-of-Work nor Proof-of-Stake; they both use a different method of validating and verifying transactions. These cryptocurrencies were developed specifically for use as payment and cross-border payment networks, and they fulfil those roles very well.

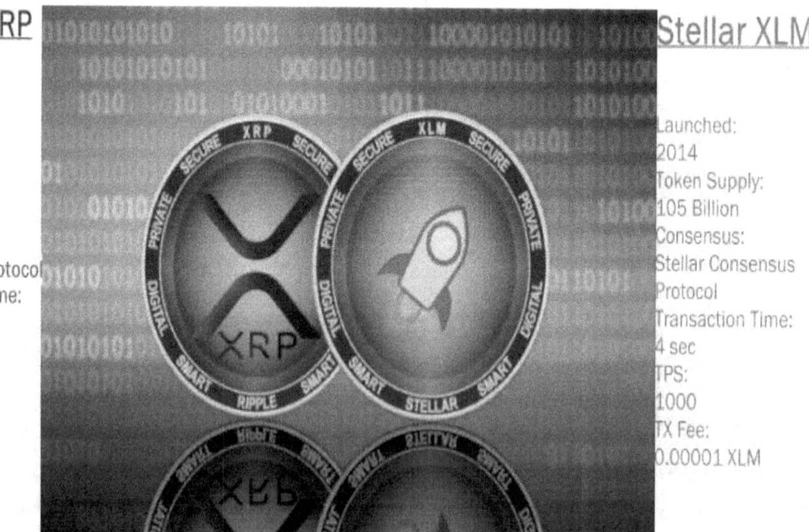

Ripple uses **Ripple Protocol Consensus Algorithms (RPCA)**, while Stellar uses the Stellar Consensus Protocol (SCP). These networks are very similar, and I won't get into the details of how they work, but basically, users can send Ripple and Stellar, or any crypto that uses that style of consensus algorithm for fractions of cents, fees so low they may as well be free which is why there are so many XRP enthusiasts. Who doesn't love essentially free transactions?

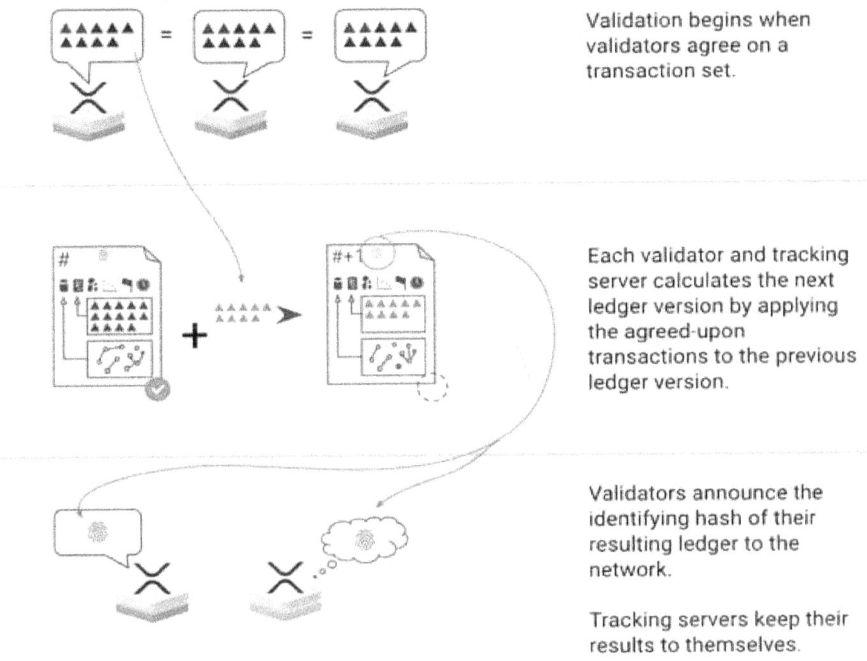

Ripple XRP's Transaction Consensus, Calculating a Ledger Validation. Image via XRPL.ORG

"Hey! We said No Fees!?"

I promise there are a couple of unique networks out there where users can send crypto completely free. The two most popular are the EOS network with the native token EOS and the Tron network, with the native token being Tron (TRX).

These networks do not use Proof-of-Work or Proof-of-Stake either; they use what is known as a *Delegated Proof-of-Stake (DPoS)* consensus mechanism. This is how users can send their Tron or EOS tokens completely free of charge if they are sending from a wallet or decentralized platform that supports these network's unique functions. Note that most exchanges may still charge a transaction fee as they always want their cut. Here is a great diagram from Blockchain Zoo breaking down the Delegated Proof-of-Stake consensus algorithm:

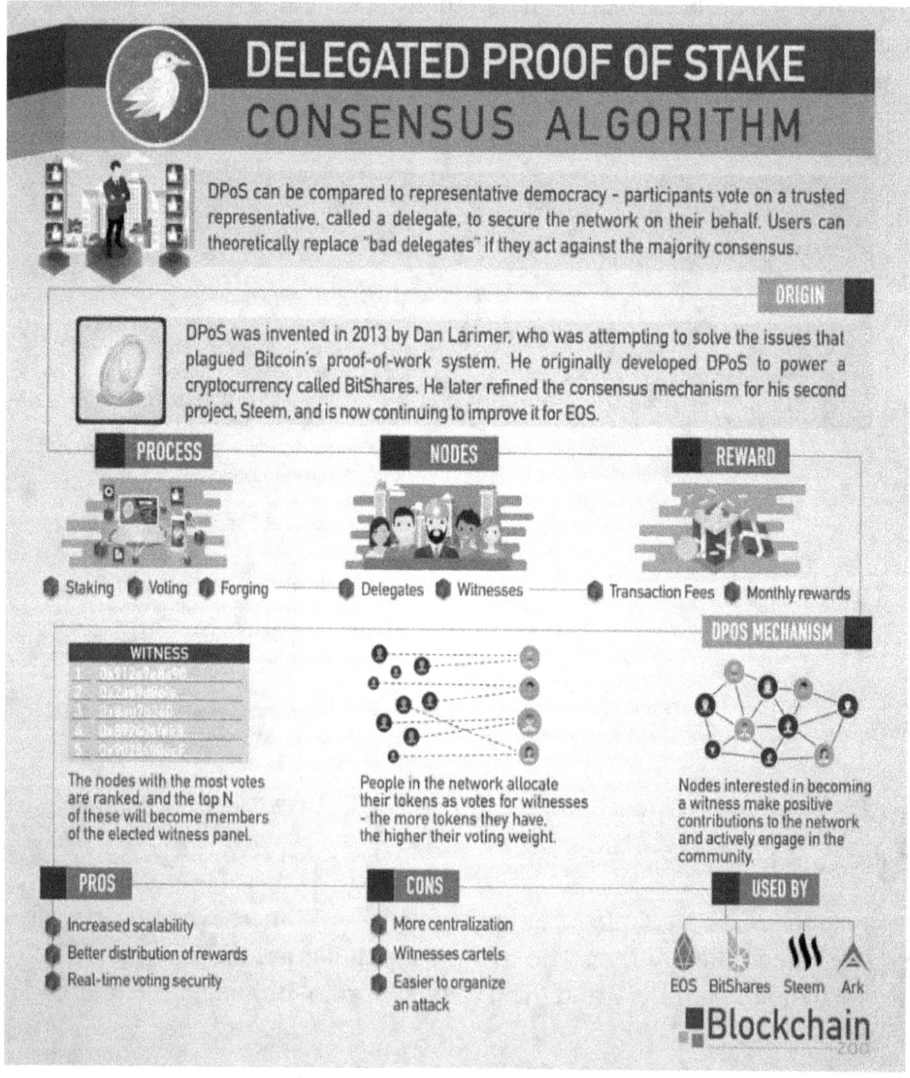

Transactions on these networks are not paid in fees but in computational power in bandwidth and CPU. These networks are not as common or as popular today as the standard Proof-of-Stake networks. However, in previous years both Tron and EOS were top ten cryptocurrency projects.

Both networks are still quite large and in use, but they have fallen out of favour in recent times due to a lack of marketing efforts and partnerships and a lack of new developer attraction. But don't write these networks off! They have been around for a long time, and some bullish projects are building out on both, such as the Bullish EOS-powered exchange backed by Peter Thiel and Block.one.

EOS-Powered Exchange backed by Block.one, Peter Thiel, Founders Fund, Galaxy, Nomura, and more

Earlier this year, **Bullish raised more than US$10 billion** in cash and digital assets first from Block.one (US$100 million, 164,000 BTC, and 20 million EOS) and then from a US$300 million strategic investment round led by Peter Thiel's Thiel Capital.

Other leading investors include Founders Fund, Alan Howard, Louis Bacon, Richard Li, Christian Angermayer, Galaxy Digital, and global investment bank Nomura, many of whom will serve as senior advisors to the company.

Bullish uses EOSIO and the EOS Public Blockchain and claims to be the first to bring externally verifiable state integrity to a high-performance trading and asset management platform.

Image via financefeeds

The way users can transact for free is to freeze or lend out their tokens to the network and get paid in return with the computational power needed to send these transactions for free. So instead of Proof-of-Stake, where validators are paid in tokens, Tron and EOS pay for "staking" in computational power for some sweet fee-free transaction action.

That is, of course, a very simplistic overview of how these networks function that does not do the ingenuity of the network creators justice for their work, but that covers the gist of it for laypeople. As these networks are slightly less "beginner-friendly," I would highly encourage you to do your homework on understanding how these DPOS networks function before diving in.

How to Save on Fees

Okay, now, for the good part, let's save you some digital cash!

I look at crypto through quite a simplistic view. Too simplistic, probably.

When I look at making purchases with crypto, I never even bother trying to use Bitcoin or Ethereum. The fees are too high, and those tokens are too valuable, in my opinion, to waste on my gummy bear purchases. To use crypto as cash, see if they accept payments in the cheapest cryptos like Ripple or Stellar. If you want to use Bitcoin, see if there is support for the **Bitcoin Lightning network**, as that is a serious game-changer that drastically reduces fees.

Dash and Litecoin are also fantastic alternatives, and Litecoin is almost as widely accepted as Bitcoin. Dogecoin is also becoming more widely accepted and has cheaper transactions than Bitcoin. Finally, look at Cardano's ADA, Solana's SOL, Avalanches' AVAX or Algorand's ALGO for transactions, as they can often be below a cent, anything to avoid BTC or ETH, really.

Be careful with Bitcoin fees as well. During **low congestion times**, a Bitcoin transaction may only cost a few cents, but fees have spiked to above 50 dollars in the past during bull run mania. Also, make sure you understand your Satoshi's and don't let all those 0's fool you into thinking it's cheap. For example, many centralized exchanges will "only" charge 0.0006 BTC for a withdrawal, but that is over 20 dollars at current Bitcoin prices!

For Bitcoin:

Use **the lightning network** when possible.

Try and reduce the frequency of Bitcoin transactions. For example, if you practice dollar-cost averaging (DCA) and frequently purchase Bitcoin on an exchange, limit the number of withdrawals to your wallet to every few months or whatever you are comfortable with. If you buy 0.0006 BTC every two weeks and the withdrawal fee is 0.0003, you lose half your purchase every time you withdraw. Save up a few purchases and move the funds in larger chunks as the fee is not dependent on the amount. Be sure to check the withdrawal fees for the platform you use to buy crypto.

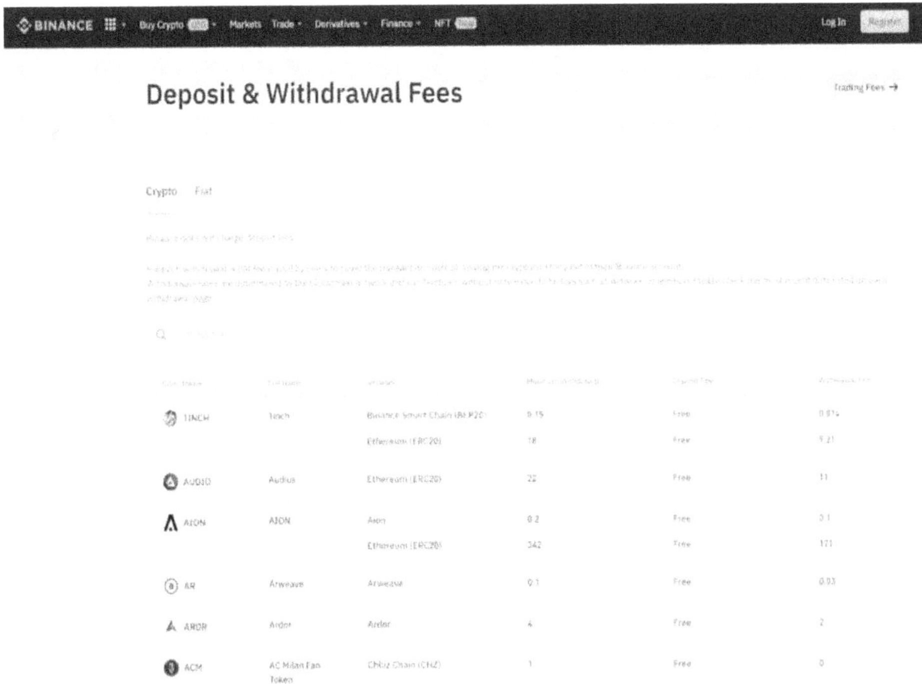

Keep an Eye on the Withdraw Fees page Image via Binance

Wait for times of lower network congestion. These times are typically on weekends, late at night, or early morning UTC. Use a site like blockchain.com and look at the **mempool** chart to see how many transactions are waiting to be confirmed. The higher the chart, the more expensive.

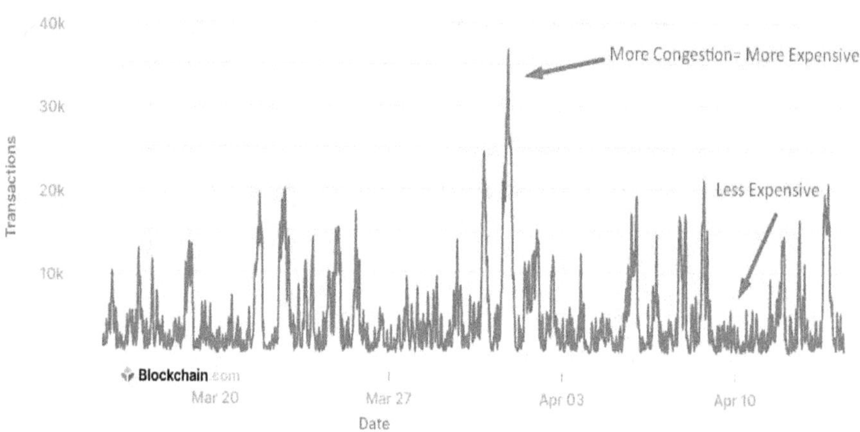

Image via blockchain.com

Adjust the fee- Most Bitcoin wallets allow you to set a custom network fee; however, if this fee is set too low, there is a chance the transaction won't get picked up or can severely slow down the transaction time. You can use a site like bitcoinfees.net that can give you recommended fees to set based on current network congestion.

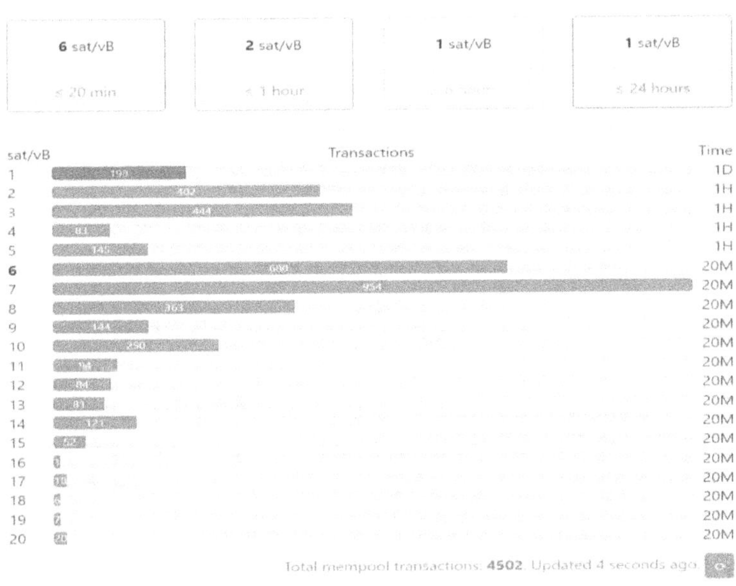

Image via Bitcoinfees

Use a wallet or platform that supports **SegWit** transactions. Using SegWit can reduce Bitcoin fees by up to 30%.

Know your Bitcoin wallet address formats. Avoid using old Bitcoin legacy addresses (P2PKH) that start with the number 1. Bitcoin addresses have evolved, as have many crypto wallets. Try and use wallets/addresses that begin with the number 3, which are Pay to Script Hash (P2SH), or even better if you can use an address that starts with bc1, which is Native SegWit (P2WPKH), as this can reduce fees up to an additional 38%.

Mind the inputs and outputs! Bitcoin transactions can be more expensive to send if the amount is made up of smaller inputs. Bitcoin network fees are proportional to the size of bytes in your transaction. Bitcoin utilizes an **Unspent Transaction Output** (UTXO) model, which means you receive BTC back like "change" back for transactions. So, if you own 5 BTC and want to send 2, your wallet sends the total amount, so

5, then 3 (minus network fees) would get returned to your wallet in what is known as a change address like so:

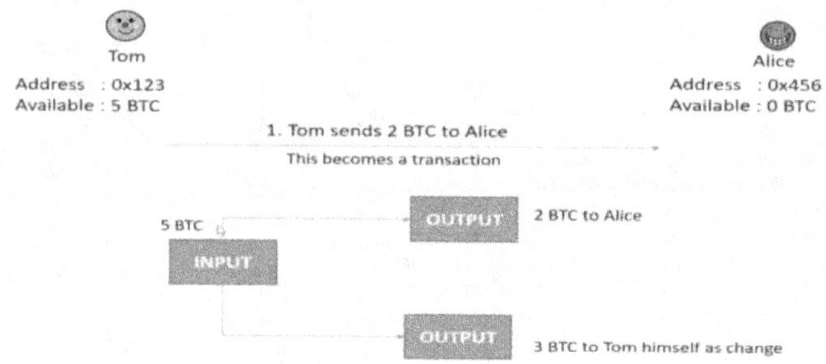

The UTXO that gets returned to the change address still appears in your wallet the same as it did before, this process can get more in-depth, and you can export your change addresses to find the bits of Bitcoin that reside in each change address if you want to, but that is a topic for another article. All this happens behind the scenes and is invisible to the user; all you need to know is that your wallet balance will reflect the proper, total balance of each change address and your Bitcoin address.

Another reason why all this is important is that if you receive multiple small Bitcoin transactions, then need to send one large transaction, the network will combine all the smaller input amounts you have received to make up the large output amount like this:

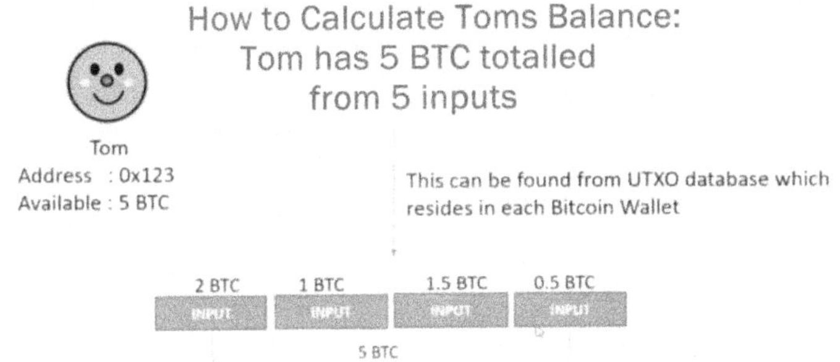

- Tom's balance is calculated in real time by the network looking up his wallet's UTXO database
- When Tom initiates a 2 BTC transfer to Alice, all the inputs are combined into a total output transaction, sending all 5 BTC, returning 3 BTC to himself
  - 2 BTC ---> Alice
  - 3 BTC ---> To himself as a UTXO

So, what this all means is if you send yourself one full Bitcoin as one transaction, then you need to send out one full Bitcoin in one transaction; that one is easy as there is one input and one output, fewer bytes of data.

Where Bitcoin fees can get expensive is if you need to send one whole Bitcoin out, but that one Bitcoin balance is made up of a bunch of smaller incoming amounts, tossed in with a few small outgoing transactions with UTXO returns, and that is now a lot of work your wallet needs to do to pile together one whole Bitcoin, resulting in a more expensive transaction.

This is analogous to say if you need to buy something for 1 dollar and you hand the cashier 1 dollar. Easy. Now say you need to buy something for 1 dollar, but you need to pay in 100 pennies, digging them all out from different pockets. Some are in your wallet, and some are in your shoes for good luck; that is a cumbersome way to pay. Bitcoin can work the same way. To avoid this, you can consider reducing the number of Bitcoin transactions you make and sending larger amounts when possible.

For Ethereum:

First and foremost, **timing is everything,** similar to Bitcoin, except that high network traffic impacts Ethereum more severely. Take a look at a site like ethgasstation.info and look at the Gwei numbers. **Gwei** is short for giga-Wei and is a denomination value for Ethereum, akin to Satoshis for

Bitcoin and cents for dollars. When this site is showing high numbers, the network is seeing a lot of traffic/congestion. The site gives three numbers to help you know how high or low to set your Ethereum gas fees. Fast on the left, which is the most expensive but will get the transaction done the quickest, standard, and slow for the penny pinchers, which will be the cheapest but also the slowest transaction time.

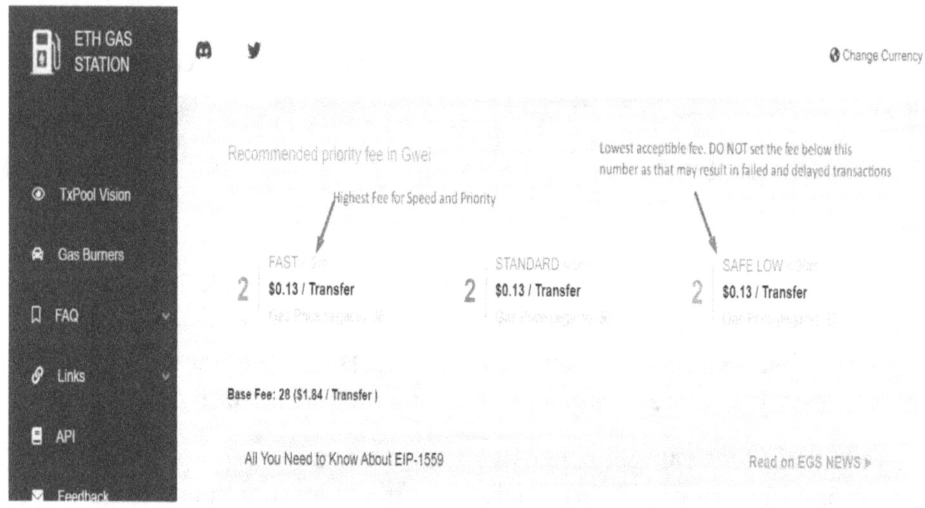

Image via ethgasstation

Most self-custody wallets like Exodus, Metamask and Trustwallet will automatically select a gas fee for you if you do not want to worry about it, but the gas fee that is automatically selected won't be the cheapest option. Most wallets will allow you to set your gas fees as an "advanced" option. As shown in the image above, avoid setting too low of a fee, don't try and set the fee below the slow number shown, as that can seriously ruin your transaction. I'm talking failed transactions and transactions that can get stuck for days.

Try and send your Ethereum transactions, which include every one of the tens of thousands of ERC20 tokens during off-peak times. Also, check sites like ethereumprice.org/gas to ensure you aren't transacting during peak times.

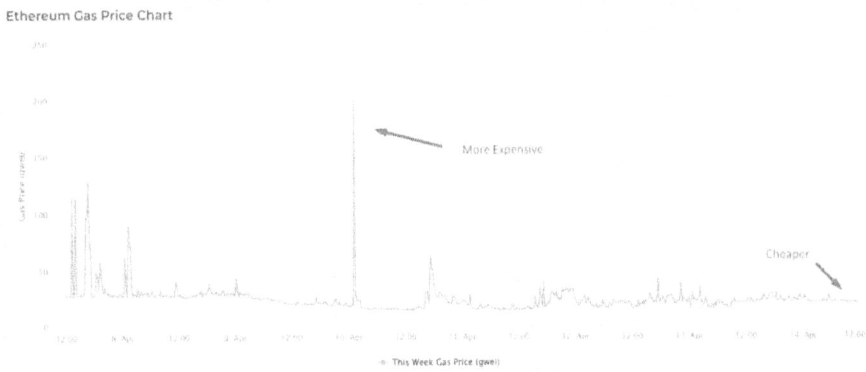

Image via ethereumprice.org

Ethereumprice.org also has a handy heat map that can help show you the cheapest times of day to transact in Ethereum, which looks like this:

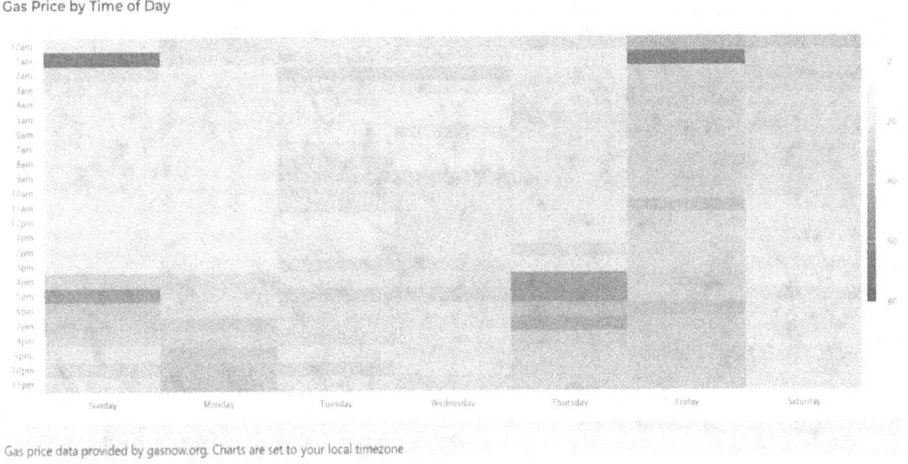

Image via Ethereumprice.org

Organize Transaction types. As with Bitcoin, try and move assets as little as possible and combine transactions to lump sums if you can, as the fee is not dependent on the amount. Gas also varies depending on the type of transaction. For example, interacting with smart contracts is often a lot pricier so avoid interacting with smart contracts if possible.

Find Decentralized applications (DAPPS) that offer discounts and reduce gas fees. Some Ethereum projects offer gas fee subsidies or minimal gas fees. Great examples of this are Balancer, KeeperDAO and Yearn's V2 vaults. They can do this by batching individual user transactions together. Aave has also made impressive strides in this area with the upgrade to Aave V2.

Utilize Gas Tokens. Users can delete their storage variables on the Ethereum network and earn ETH as refunds for doing so. You can mint the gas tokens when the gas fees are low and redeem the gas tokens for ETH, which can be used to pay gas fees. You can learn about that process on gastoken.io

Explore layer-two solutions. Layer two solutions were created out of necessity to battle the painfully high Ethereum gas fees. Most of these solutions involve moving transactions to side chains. Projects like Polygon, Loopring, OMG Network, Skale, ZK Swap, Cartesi, Optimism and Arbitrum are the primary Ethereum scaling solutions.

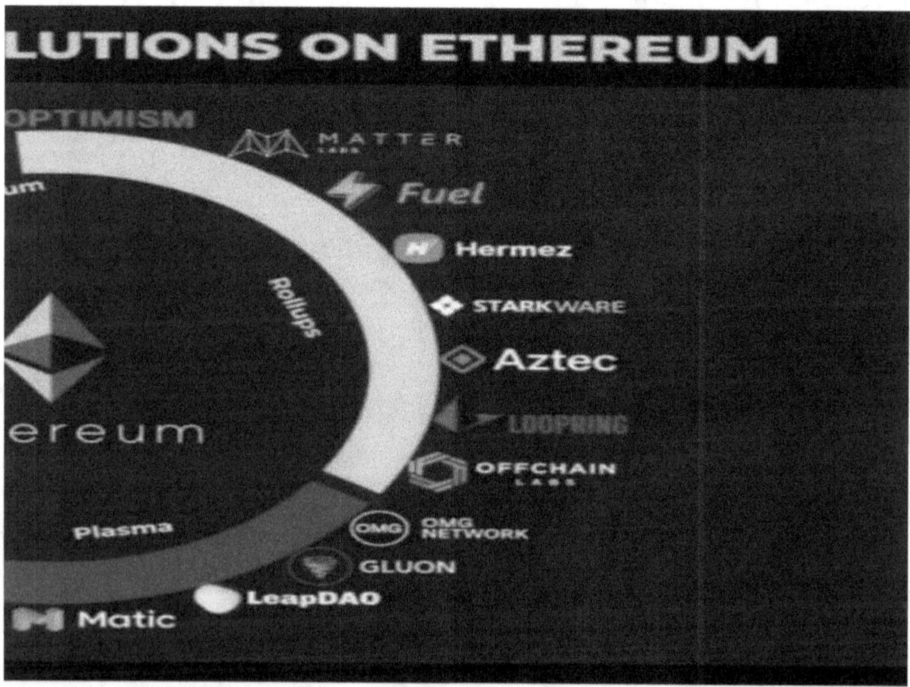

Image via Coin98 Analytics

Look for crypto platforms that utilize these scaling solutions for cheaper Ethereum alternatives like Binance Smart Chain, Cardano, Solana or Avalanche though each network has its pros and cons.

Other Crypto:

If you are using Ripple XRP, Stellar XLM, or locking away for computing power with EOS or Tron, then you don't have to worry about anything. Send XRP and XLM whenever you want with **no fuss**. Send Tron and EOS whenever you **have enough CPU resources** collected. For cheaper Proof-of-Stake protocols like Solana, Cardano, Avalanche, etc., and cheaper Proof-of-Work networks like Litecoin or Doge etc., the best thing you can do to make sure your fees are at their cheapest is to use the network during off-peak times. However, this isn't as important with other cryptos as it is with Ethereum, as price fluctuations are not as significant. When it comes to crypto, high fees can put a serious cramp on your crypto party, but following the steps in this article, you can save yourself potentially hundreds of dollars in fees for just a few extra steps. I use the Eth gas station every time I send an Ethereum transaction and always set it to the lowest safe fee shown and that move alone has saved me hundreds and only takes a minute!

What is a Cryptocurrency wallet?

Cryptocurrency wallets store users' public and private keys, while providing an easy-to-use interface to manage crypto balances. They also support cryptocurrency transfers through the blockchain. Some wallets even allow users to perform certain actions with their crypto assets, such as buying and selling or interacting with decentralised applications (dapps).

It is important to remember that cryptocurrency transactions do not represent a 'sending' of crypto tokens from a person's mobile phone to someone else's mobile phone. When sending tokens, a user's private key signs the transaction and broadcasts it to the blockchain network. The network then includes the transaction to reflect the updated balance in both the sender's and recipient's address.

So, the term 'wallet' is somewhat of a misnomer, as crypto wallets don't actually store cryptocurrency in the same way physical wallets hold cash. Instead, they read the public ledger to show the balances in a user's addresses, as well as hold **the private keys** that enable the user to make transactions.

Not sure what a Public or Private Key is?

We will see about public and private keys later on the topic Blockchain 101 but for your convenience I will give you quick explanation.
A key is a long string of random, unpredictable characters. While a **public key** is like a bank account number and can be shared widely, the **private key** is like a bank account password or PIN and should be kept secret. In public-key cryptography, every public key is paired with one corresponding private key. Together, they are used to encrypt and decrypt data.

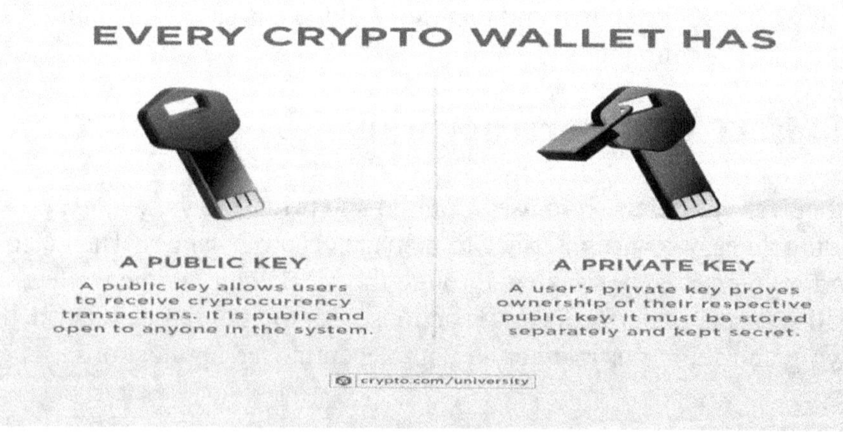

How Do Cryptocurrency Wallets Work?

As mentioned earlier, a wallet doesn't technically hold a user's coins. Instead, it holds the key to their coins, which are stored on public blockchain networks.

In order to perform various transactions, a user needs to verify their address via a private key that comes in a set of specific codes. The speed and security often depend on the kind of wallet a user has.

Different Types of Crypto Wallets

There are two main types of crypto wallets: software-based hot wallets and physical cold wallets.
Hot and Cold Wallets — What's the Difference?

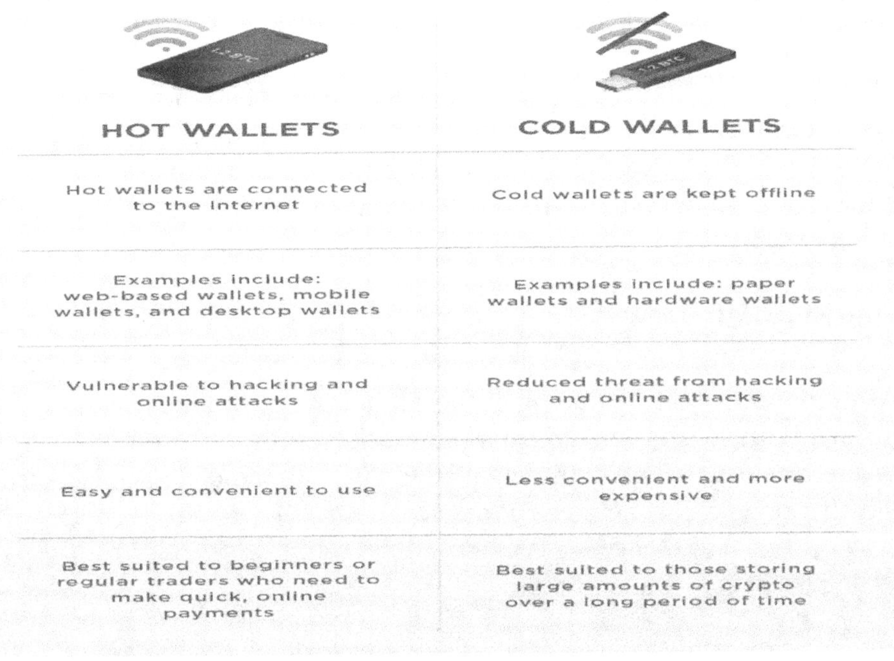

Hot Wallets

The main difference between hot and cold wallets is whether they are connected to the Internet. Hot wallets are connected to the Internet, while cold wallets are kept offline. This means that funds stored in hot wallets are more accessible and, therefore, easier for hackers to gain access to.

Examples of hot wallets include:

- Web-based wallets
- Mobile wallets
- Desktop wallets

In hot wallets, private keys are stored and encrypted on the app itself, which is kept online. Using a hot wallet can be risky since computer networks have hidden vulnerabilities that can be targeted by hackers or malware programs to break into the system. Keeping large amounts of cryptocurrency in a hot wallet is a fundamentally poor security practice, but the risks can be mitigated by using a hot wallet with stronger encryption, or by using devices that store private keys in a secure enclave.

There are different reasons why a market participant might want their cryptocurrency holdings to be either connected to or disconnected from the Internet. Because of this, it's not uncommon for cryptocurrency holders to have multiple cryptocurrency wallets, including both hot and cold ones.

Cold Wallets

As introduced at the beginning of this section, a cold wallet is entirely offline. While not as convenient as hot wallets, cold wallets are far more secure. An example of a physical medium used for cold storage is a piece of paper or an engraved piece of metal.

Examples of cold wallets include:

- Paper wallets
- Hardware wallets

What is a Paper Wallet?

A paper wallet is a physical location where the private and public keys are written down or printed. In many ways, this is safer than keeping funds in a hot wallet, since remote hackers have no way of accessing these keys, which are kept safe from phishing attacks. On the other hand, it opens up the potential risk of the piece of paper getting destroyed or lost, which may result in irrecoverable funds.

What is a Hardware Wallet?

A hardware wallet is an external accessory (usually a USB or Bluetooth device) that stores a user's keys; a user can only sign a transaction by pushing a physical button on the device, which malicious actors cannot control.

The best practice to store cryptocurrency assets that do not require instant access is offline in a cold wallet. However, users should note this also means that securing their assets is entirely their own responsibility   it is up to them to ensure they don't lose it, or have it stolen.

Tip: For increased security, separate the public and private keys, keep them offline, and store the physical wallet in a safe deposit box.

Custodial and Non-Custodial Wallets

In addition to those mentioned above, wallets can be further separated into custodial and non-custodial types.

CUSTODIAL	NON-CUSTODIAL
...or third party has ...he private keys	Users have complete control of their private keys and funds
...ure, as funds ...d online and ...e vulnerable ...acking	More secure, as users hold their private keys offline
...al responsibility ...es trust in the ...that holds user ...unds	Users are wholly responsible for keeping their funds and private keys secure
...lace, so if users ...rivate key, they ...egain access to ...r wallet	If users lose their private keys or recovery passwords, then they lose access to their funds
...y KYC and ...rocedures	No KYC or AML procedures
...ser-friendly	Less user-friendly
...d to beginners ...arting out	Best suited to those who want to retain full control of their funds

Custodial Wallets

Most web-based crypto wallets tend to be custodial wallets. Typically offered on cryptocurrency exchanges, these wallets are known for their convenience and ease of usage, and are especially popular with newcomers, as well as experienced day traders.

The main difference between custodial wallets and the types mentioned above is that users are no longer in full control of their tokens, and the private keys needed to sign for transactions are held only by the exchange.

The implication here is that users must trust the service provider to securely store their tokens and implement strong security measures to prevent unauthorised access. These measures include two-factor authentication (2FA), email confirmation, and biometric authentication, such as facial recognition or fingerprint verification. Many exchanges will not allow a user to make transactions until these security measures are properly set up.

Exchanges and custodial wallet providers usually also take further steps to ensure the safety of users' tokens. For example, a portion of the funds is generally transferred to the company's cold wallet, safe from online attackers.

Crypto.com has taken many measures to ensure the protection of customer funds. After rigorous security audits by a team of cybersecurity and compliance experts, Crypto.com is the first crypto company in the world to have obtained ISO/IEC 27701:2019, ISO22301:2019, ISO27001:2013, and PCI:DSS 3.2.1, Level 1 compliance, and independently assessed at Tier 4, the highest level for both NIST Cybersecurity and Privacy Frameworks, as well as Service Organization Control (SOC) 2 compliance.

Additionally, the company has in place a total of US$360 million for insurance protection of customer funds.

Non-Custodial Wallets

Non-custodial wallets, on the other hand, allow a user to retain full control of their funds, since the private key is stored locally with the user.

When starting a non-custodial wallet, the user is asked to write down and safely store a list of 12 randomly generated words, known as a 'recovery', 'seed', or 'mnemonic' phrase. From this phrase, the user's public and private keys can be generated. This acts as a backup or recovery mechanism in case the user loses access to their device.

Anyone with the seed phrase is able to gain full control of the funds held in that wallet. In a case scenario where the seed phrase is lost, the user also loses access to their funds. So it is imperative to keep the mnemonic phrase in a secure location, and to not store a digital copy of it anywhere. Do not print it out at a public printer or take a picture of it.

Note that hardware wallets are inherently non-custodial, since private keys are stored on the device itself. There are also software-based non-custodial wallets, such as the Crypto.com DeFi Wallet. The common theme is that the private keys and the funds are fully in the user's control. As the popular saying within the crypto community goes, 'not your keys, not your coins!'.

On the flip side, this means that users must be in charge of their own security with regard to the storage of passwords and seed phrases. If any of these are lost, recovery can be difficult or impossible because they are typically not stored on any third-party server.

Custodial vs Non-Custodial Wallets: Which Are Better?

Custodial and non-custodial wallets have various pros and cons that make them suitable for different types of users:
For those prone to losing passwords and devices, then it makes sense to use a custodial wallet, since an exchange or custodian is likely to have better security practices and backup options. That's why it's a popular option for beginners who have little to no experience trading crypto. Further, transaction fees with a custodial wallet tend to be cheaper or even free.
However, for those who prefer to retain full control over their own funds, consider a non-custodial wallet.
Ultimately, it all comes down to personal choice.

For Additional Security, Consider **Multi-Signature Wallets**
Multi-signature wallets — or multisig wallets — require two or more private key signatures to authorise transactions. This solution is useful for a number of use cases:

An individual using a multisig wallet can prevent losing access to the entire wallet in a case scenario where one key is lost. For example, if a user loses one key, there will still be two other keys able to sign transactions.

Multisig wallets can prevent the misuse of funds and fraud, which makes them a good option for hedge funds, exchanges, and corporations. Since each authorised person has one key, and a sign-off requires the majority of keys, it becomes impossible for any individual to unilaterally make unauthorised transactions.

Any of the wallet types described above have multisig versions — multisig hot wallets, cold wallets, hardware wallets, etc.

NFT Wallets

An NFT wallet is a secure place that stores non-fungible tokens (NFTs). For NFT wallets, there are two main choices: hardware wallets or software-based wallets.

What to Look for in an NFT Wallet

The right NFT wallet depends on a variety of factors, including a user's level of experience and security needs, as well as the types of tokens they plan on storing. Here are some things to consider when choosing an NFT wallet:

- **Compatibility with NFT marketplaces** — User needs a wallet that can integrate with the NFT marketplaces they want to buy from.
- **Strong security** — Can include two-factor authentication (2FA), email confirmation, or biometric authentication.
- **User-friendly interface** — A good NFT wallet should boast a streamlined user experience, and be easy to set up.
- **Accessibility on multiple devices** — Most NFT wallets are available via web extensions or as mobile/desktop applications. For enhanced convenience, look for a wallet that's available on multiple devices that can also synchronise transactions in real time.
- **Cross-chain compatibility** — Most wallets support Ethereum-based tokens; however, for those who want to mint, buy, and sell

tokens on other networks, a wallet with cross-chain compatibility is needed.

Popular hardware wallets include devices by Ledger and Trezor. However, as NFTs are not natively supported by either of these wallets, users need to connect their hardware wallet to a hot wallet that's capable of storing and managing NFTs.

For an all-in-one solution, consider the Crypto.com DeFi Wallet, widely regarded as one of the most trusted and secure wallets to store NFTs — and voted the best NFT wallet 2022 by TradingPlatforms.

More about Crypto.com DeFi Wallet
The Crypto.com DeFi Wallet is non-custodial, which means that users retain full control of their private keys and assets. Available on Android and iOS, DeFi Wallet allows users to manage 700-plus tokens across 20-plus blockchains and send crypto to anyone at their preferred confirmation speed and network fee.

What's more, the dedicated wallet supports NFTs on Ethereum, Cronos, and Crypto.org Chain, and enables users to easily view top collections using the NFT Spotlight feature. Users can also use the wallet to potentially earn passive income by locking up cryptocurrencies like CRO, USDC, and DOT. Crypto.com users can now also choose to manage their NFTs within the Crypto.com App.

Security in the Cryptoverse

One of the biggest concerns with cryptocurrency investing is how safe cryptocurrency is, as well as how the evolving world of regulations may impact different platforms and opportunities worldwide.

How safe is crypto?

When investors ask about security and crypto, there are a few angles to this question. The first is that while crypto is secure in that it's built on the principles of cryptography and peer-to-peer consensus, many cryptocurrencies — especially in the early days — have been beset by hacks, theft, and other forms of cyber-attacks. These aren't common, but they are a potential risk to consider.

Then there's the issue of how to secure the crypto you buy. To store crypto securely, an investor needs to use a cryptocurrency wallet: either a digital wallet or a physical means of storage like a thumb drive. When using a crypto wallet, you will be relied on to store, remember, and secure a password that only you know. This is frequently an issue with crypto, as people who forget their passwords essentially have had their assets stranded. Crypto wallets may also be vulnerable to hacks.

Last, investors have to consider the overall risks of trading an investment as volatile as most cryptocurrencies can be. Crypto values can fluctuate by the day, the hour, the minute. And while that's also true of some traditional investments, particularly equities, cryptocurrencies are so new that the sector as a whole doesn't have much of a track record that investors can consider when making investment choices.

Cryptocurrency Rules and Regulations

While cryptocurrency has become much easier to buy and sell thanks to widespread interest in it from the general public, the cryptocurrency rules and regulations are less well established than they are for other types of assets or currencies like stocks or dollars. This is true in the U.S. and in countries around the world, many of which are still determining whether to sanction the use of cryptocurrencies at all, and if they do, how to regulate them. The Securities and Exchange Commission (SEC), which regulates the trading of many financial assets, has basically split the cryptocurrency world into two, ruling that bitcoin is a "payment mechanism and store of value," i.e. not a security like a stock or bond, which come under much more strict scrutiny from the SEC.
Many "tokens," cryptocurrencies issued by companies to fund or pre-fund a business project, do fall under the SEC's definition of "security" and thus face much tighter regulation. It's wise to keep an eye on how regulatory issues are evolving in this space, as changes to existing rules can have a substantial impact on investments. But it's clear that

cryptocurrency will be the future business and legalized everywhere with applied governmental regulations and taxations.

***

Blockchain 101

What is blockchain technology? What makes it so important?

For many, blockchain technology is still a mysterious or even intimidating topic. Some even remain skeptical that we'll use this technology in the future. This skepticism that exists today is understandable because we're still very early in the development and widespread adoption of blockchain technology.

These times is to blockchain what the late 1990s were to the internet. And like the internet, blockchain technology is anything but a fad, it's here to stay, and if you're reading this, you're early too.

This article demystifies blockchain technology. This is your 'intro to blockchain technology 101'. A complete, easy-to-understand, step by step beginners blockchain breakdown. You'll learn everything from what blockchain is and why it matters, to how blockchain works (step by step) and what today – tomorrow's – most promising blockchain applications may be.

You'll also walk away from this article confidently, and well on your way to making informed, independent blockchain technology investment decisions. And you'll be no slouch if you want to hold your own in conversations with family and friends too!

So, let's dive in!

Blockchain technology is the concept or protocol behind the running of the blockchain. Blockchain technology makes cryptocurrencies (digital currencies secured by cryptography) like Bitcoin work just like the internet makes email possible.

The blockchain is an **immutable** (unchangeable, meaning a transaction or file recorded cannot be changed) **distributed digital ledger** (digital record of transactions or data stored in multiple places on a computer network) with many use cases beyond cryptocurrencies.

Immutable and distributed are two fundamental blockchain properties. The immutability of the ledger means you can always trust it to be accurate. Being distributed protects the blockchain from network attacks.

Each transaction or record on the ledger is stored in a "block." For example, blocks on the Bitcoin blockchain consist of an average of more than 500 Bitcoin transactions.

The Information contained in a block is dependent on and linked to the information in a previous block and, over time, forms a chain of transactions, Hence the word *blockchain!*

Types of Blockchains

There are four types of blockchains:

1. Public Blockchains

Public blockchains are open, decentralized networks of computers accessible to anyone wanting to request or validate a transaction (check for accuracy). Those (miners) who validate transactions receive rewards. Public blockchains use proof-of-work or proof-of-stake consensus mechanisms (discussed later). Two common examples of public blockchains include the Bitcoin and Ethereum (ETH) blockchains.

2. Private Blockchains

Private blockchains are not open, they have access restrictions. People who want to join require permission from the system administrator. They are typically governed by one entity, meaning they're centralized. For example, Hyperledger is a private, permissioned blockchain.

3. Hybrid Blockchains or Consortiums

Consortiums are a combination of public and private blockchains and contain centralized and decentralized features. For example, Energy Web Foundation, Dragonchain, and R3.

Take note: There isn't a 100 percent consensus on whether these are different terms. Some make a distinction between the two, while others consider them the same thing.

4. Sidechains

A sidechain is a blockchain running parallel to the main chain. It allows users to move digital assets between two different blockchains and improves scalability and efficiency. An example of a sidechain is the *Liquid Network*.

History of Blockchain

Blockchain isn't just a database, it's a new technology stack with 'digital trust' that is revolutionizing the way we exchange value and information across the internet, by taking out the 'gatekeepers' from the process. Blockchain history goes back farther than you might imagine, but i've condensed it by answering four critical questions:

Who invented Blockchain?

The first blockchain-like protocol was proposed by cryptographer David Chaum in 1982. Later in 1991, Stuart Haber and W. Scott Stornetta wrote about their work on Consortiums.

But it was **Satoshi Nakamoto** (presumed pseudonym for a person or group of people) who invented and implemented the first blockchain network after deploying the world's first digital currency, Bitcoin. **Cryptography** is a deep and fascinating discipline with a history that goes back further than blockchain.

Who owns Blockchain Technology?

Because blockchain technology is the technology behind the blockchain, it cannot be owned. It's like the internet. But anyone can use the technology to run and own their own blockchains.

Who founded Bitcoin?

Satoshi Nakamoto.

Who sent and received the first Bitcoin Transaction?

Nakamoto sent ten bitcoins to Hal Finney, who built the first reusable proof-of-work system in 2004.

How does a Public Blockchain work?

Let's start with an oversimplification.

As a society, we created ledgers to store information—and they have a variety of applications. For example, we use ledgers in real estate to store a house's records, such as when alterations were made or the house was sold. We also use ledgers in **bookkeeping** to record all the transactions a company makes.

Bookkeeping mostly relies on double-entry accounting to store transactions. Although this is a step-up from single-entry accounting that lacks transparency and accountability, double-entry accounting also has its pitfalls: Entries are accounted for separately, making it difficult for one counterparty to verify the other's records.

Records stored using traditional ledgers are also easy to tamper with, meaning you can easily edit, remove, or add a record. As a result, you're less likely to trust that the information is accurate.

Public blockchains solve both these problems – and the way we trust – by evolving the traditional bookkeeping model to triple-entry bookkeeping: transactions on a blockchain are cryptographically sealed by a third entry. This creates a tamper-proof record of transactions stored in blocks and verified by a distributed consensus mechanism.

These consensus mechanisms also ensure new blocks get added to any blockchain. An example of a consensus mechanism is proof-of-work (PoW), often referred to as "mining."

Mining isn't universal to all blockchains; it's just one type of consensus mechanism currently used by Bitcoin and some others.

Here's how this process works with Bitcoin. When sending Bitcoin, you pay a small fee (in bitcoin) for a network of computers to confirm your transaction is valid. Your transaction is then bundled with other transactions pending in a queue to be added to a new block.

The computers (nodes) then work to validate this list of transactions in the block by solving a complex mathematical problem to come up with a hash, which is a 64-digit hexadecimal number.

Once solved, the block is added to the network—and your fee, combined with all other transaction fees in that block, is the miner's reward. It's that simple.

Each new block added to the network is assigned a unique key (via cryptography). To obtain each new key, the previous block's key and information are inputted into a formula.

As new blocks are continually added through the ongoing mining process, they become increasingly secure and harder to tamper with. Anyone caught trying to edit a record will simply be ignored. All future blocks then depend on information from prior blocks—and this dependency from one block to the next forms a secure chain: **the blockchain.**

You can see this depicted below for house records stored on the blockchain. For example, Block 2 provides a key after taking all the information from Block 1 into account (including the key) and inputting it into a formula. Block 3, in turn, provides a new key after taking all the information from Block 1 and Block 2 into account (including the key) and inputting it into a formula. And so, the process repeats itself indefinitely.

Now, let's dig deeper, exploring proof-of-work (PoW) vs. proof-of-stake (PoS) and the blockchain trilemma, which are fundamental to the public blockchain's functioning.

Proof of Work (PoW) vs. Proof of Stake (PoS)

A public blockchain functions through consensus mechanisms: the process for validating transactions without a third party like a bank.
PoW and PoS are two such mechanisms. While their goal—to reach a consensus that a transaction is valid—remains the same, how they get there is a little different.

What is PoW?

PoW, the technical term for mining, is the original consensus mechanism. It is still used by Bitcoin as of writing. PoW is based on cryptography, which uses mathematical equations only computers can solve.
The example in the previous section of how blocks get added to the Bitcoin Blockchain explains this system.

The two big problems with PoW are that it uses a lot of electricity and can only process a limited number of transactions simultaneously (seven for Bitcoin). Transactions typically take at least ten minutes to complete, with this delay increasing when the network is congested. Though compared to

the days-long wait required to wire money across the globe, or even to clear a check, Bitcoin's ten-minute delay is quite remarkable.
Other consensus mechanisms were created to solve these PoW problems; the most popular being PoS.

What is PoS?

PoS still uses cryptographic algorithms for validation, but transactions get validated by a chosen validator based on how many coins they hold, also known as their **stake**.

Individuals aren't technically mining, and there's no block reward. Instead, blocks are 'forged.' Those participating in this process lock a specific number of coins on the network.

The bigger a person's stake, the more mining power they have—and the higher the chances they'll be selected as the validator for the next block.

To ensure those with the most coins aren't always selected, other selection methods are used. These include **randomized block selection** (forgers with the highest stake and lowest hash value are chosen) and **coin age selection** (forgers are selected based on how long they've held their coins)

The results are faster transaction times and lower costs. The NEO and Dash cryptocurrencies, for example, can send and receive transactions in seconds.

Blockchain or Scalability Trilemma: Decentralization, Security, and Scalability

Most blockchain projects are built around three core properties: decentralization, scalability, and security. Developers are constantly trying to balance these aspects, so one isn't compromised.

But they often have to sacrifice one for the others. The 'blockchain trilemma,' concept was first coined the 'scalability trilemma' by Ethereum founder, Vitalik Buterin.

Let's look at these concepts in more detail and explore the tradeoffs:

Decentralization

Decentralization means there's no central point of control. Instead, decisions are made via consensus over a distributed network of computers.

There is, however, one significant tradeoff: speed. Sending transactions takes longer because multiple confirmations are required to validate a transaction. Hence why Bitcoin is slow.

Scalability

Scalability is the ability of the system to cope with a growing number of transactions. Scalability is crucial for mass adoption because any system needs to operate efficiently as more people use it.

Below is a rough breakdown of how many transactions Ethereum, Bitcoin, and credit card companies can process per second:

Bitcoin: *7 per second*
Ethereum: *30 per second*
Credit cards: *5,000 credit* card transactions per second with the ability to process much more if needed. Visa, for example, can process up to 24,000 transactions per second.

But achieving scalability often comes at the expense of decentralization. EOS, for example, promises a maximum of 4000 TPS but has come under criticism for being too centralized.

Security

Security is the ability of a blockchain to be protected from attacks. Unfortunately, exchanges and source code have been hacked on many occasions, suggesting that many developers focus on scalability and decentralization at the expense of security. So, you can understand that these three conditions can't be fulfilled at the same time but most of time 2 out of the 3 Blockchain trilemma. If there is high speed transaction (Scalability) then it should be at the expense of Decentralization and the reverse is the same too.

Now let's see some important concept in Blockchain…what are blockchain public and private keys?

Blockchain Consensus Mechanism

Consensus mechanisms are a critical component of blockchain technology, as they enable a decentralized network of nodes to agree on a single version of the truth without the need for a trusted third party. There are several different consensus mechanisms used in blockchain, each with its own strengths and weaknesses. Below are some of the most common consensus mechanisms used in blockchain along with PoW and PoS that I already explained.

1. Proof of Work (PoW)

Proof of Work is the original consensus algorithm used in Bitcoin. In PoW, nodes compete to solve complex mathematical problems in order to validate transactions and add new blocks to the blockchain. The first node to solve the problem and add a block to the chain is rewarded with newly minted cryptocurrency. PoW is highly secure, but it is also very energy-intensive and slow.

2. Proof of Stake (PoS)

Proof of Stake is an alternative to PoW that aims to reduce the energy consumption required to validate transactions. In PoS, nodes are chosen to validate transactions based on the amount of cryptocurrency they hold. The more cryptocurrency a node holds, the more likely it is to be chosen to validate transactions. PoS is faster and less energy-intensive than PoW, but it is also more vulnerable to certain types of attacks.

3. Delegated Proof of Stake (DPoS)

Delegated Proof of Stake is similar to PoS, but instead of all nodes being able to participate in the validation process, a smaller group of nodes is chosen to validate transactions on behalf of the network. These nodes are typically chosen by the community through a voting process. DPoS is faster and more energy-efficient than PoW or PoS, but it is also more centralized.

4. Proof of Authority (PoA)

Proof of Authority is a consensus mechanism that is commonly used in private or consortium blockchains. In PoA, a group of pre-approved nodes is chosen to validate transactions on the network. These nodes are trusted members of the network, and their identities are known to all participants. PoA is fast and efficient, but it is also highly centralized and vulnerable to attacks if one or more of the approved nodes are compromised.

5. Proof of Elapsed Time (PoET)

Proof of Elapsed Time is a consensus mechanism used in the Hyperledger Sawtooth blockchain. In PoET, nodes are randomly chosen to validate transactions based on a randomly generated wait time. The node with the shortest wait time is chosen to validate the transaction. PoET is energy-efficient and secure, but it is also vulnerable to certain types of attacks.

6. Proof of Capacity (PoC)

Proof of Capacity is a consensus mechanism used in the Burstcoin blockchain. In PoC, nodes compete to validate transactions based on the amount of storage capacity they have rather than computational power. The more storage a node has, the more likely it is to be chosen to validate transactions. PoC is energy-efficient and secure, but it requires a large amount of storage capacity.

As I told you each has its own strengths and weaknesses, and the choice of which mechanism to use depends on the specific use case and requirements of the network.

Blockchain Public & Private Key

The field of cryptography is fundamental to many cryptocurrency systems such as Bitcoin. Cryptography is the practice of secure communication in the presence of third parties. In other words, cryptography allows for data to be stored and communicated in such a way that third parties are prevented from reading the contents of what has been communicated. Cryptography is utilized in the creation of a public keys and private keys to make cryptocurrency systems a secure network upon which users can safely operate.

The concept of ownership in a cryptocurrency system revolves around three interconnected elements:

- Digital keys (Public Key and Private key)
- Cryptocurrency addresses
- Digital signatures.

Among these elements, digital keys hold the utmost significance as they enable the ownership features found in cryptographically secure cryptocurrency systems. It's crucial to understand that these digital keys are not stored within the cryptocurrency networks themselves. Instead, they are created and stored by cryptocurrency wallets, which exist independently of the network.

Digital keys are generated in pairs, comprising a public key and **a private key**. The public key serves as an individual's bank account, while the private key functions as the secret PIN to access that bank account.

The public key and cryptocurrency address are closely linked in a cryptographic manner. The cryptocurrency address is derived from the public key and acts as a representation of it. Typically, the public key is utilized to generate the actual cryptocurrency address. This address functions as a unique identifier for a user's account, enabling funds to be received and deposited into it.

Public Key

The important aspect to understand about the incorporation of public key cryptography in cryptocurrency systems such as Bitcoin, is that they are practically irreversible. This means that the mathematical functions that constitute public key cryptography are relatively easy to calculate in one direction, and are practically impossible to calculate in the opposite direction. This cryptographic feature is at the heart of cryptocurrency systems, because it facilitates the creation of digital secrets and unforgeable digital signatures that are essential for ownership on these decentralized networks.

Cryptocurrencies such as Bitcoin utilize **elliptic curve multiplication** as the foundation for their cryptography. Elliptic curve point multiplication is the operation of successively adding a point along an elliptic curve to itself repeatedly. It is used in elliptic curve cryptography as a means of producing a **one-way function**, which is a function that is easy to compute in one direction, but difficult to do so in the opposite direction. In cryptocurrency systems such as Bitcoin, this one-way function takes the private key as an input to generate the public key, which is the output.

Because of this, owners of a private key can confidently distribute their public key with the knowledge that no one will be able to reverse the function and calculate the private key from the public key.

Cryptocurrency Addresses

A cryptocurrency address is simply a string of alphanumerical characters that a user can share with anyone that wants to send them money. As mentioned before, **a cryptocurrency address** is effectively a representation of the public key. An address is derived from the public key through the use of a one-way cryptographic hash function. With Bitcoin, the algorithms that are used to make a bitcoin address from the public key are the Secure Hash Algorithm 256 (SHA-256) and the RACE Integrity Primitives Evaluation Message Digest 160 (RIPEMD-160).

Beginning with the public key, this string of values is first ran through the SHA-256 hashing algorithm to produce a hash, and then that hash is computed using RIPEMD160 to produce a bitcoin address. The bitcoin address, and addresses in other cryptocurrency systems, are what often appears in a transaction between two parties, with the address signifying the recipient of the funds.

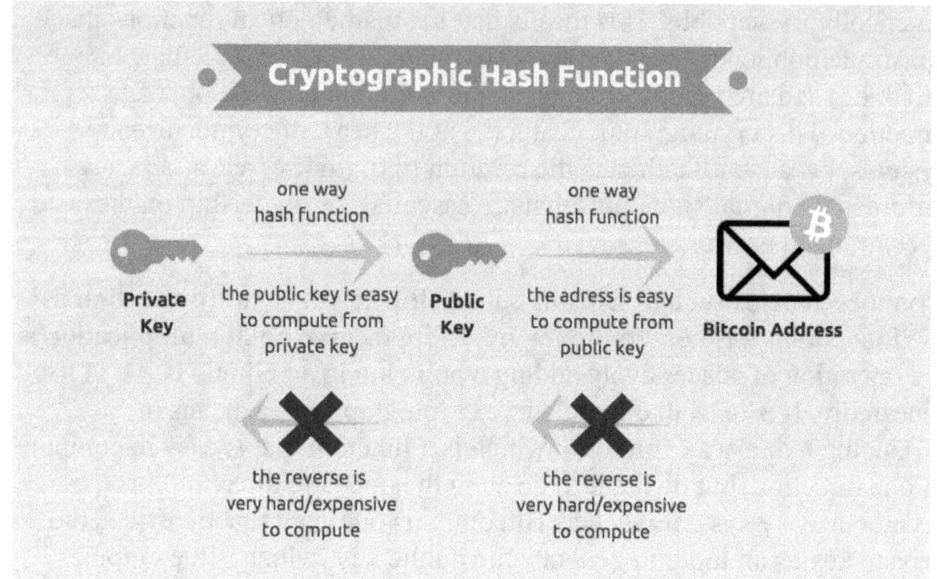

Private Keys

The private key consists of alphanumerical characters that give a user access and control over their funds to their corresponding cryptocurrency address. The private key is used to sign transactions that allow the user to spend their funds. In other words, the private key creates unique digital signatures for every transaction that enable a user to spend their funds, by proving that the user does in fact have ownership of those funds.

For example:

When Bob decides to buy a coffee from Alice's store using 5 bitcoins, he provides his public key and a digital signature generated by applying his private key to the transaction. The **digital signature** is a unique cryptographic proof that can only be generated by someone with knowledge of the private key, which is Bob in this case.

However, anyone with access to the public key and digital signature can use these elements to verify that Bob is the legitimate owner of the 5 bitcoins. This verification process allows all other participants on the

Bitcoin network to validate and accept Bob's transaction as authentic without requiring Bob's private key to be disclosed.

Digital Signatures

A digital signature is a mathematical scheme that is used for showing the authenticity of a digital message or document. A digital signature that is valid will give the recipient of a digital message or document reason to believe that the message or document was in fact created by a known sender. A digital signature also indicates that the sender cannot in any way deny having sent the message or document, and that the message or document was not altered at any point while it was in transit.

Digital Signature

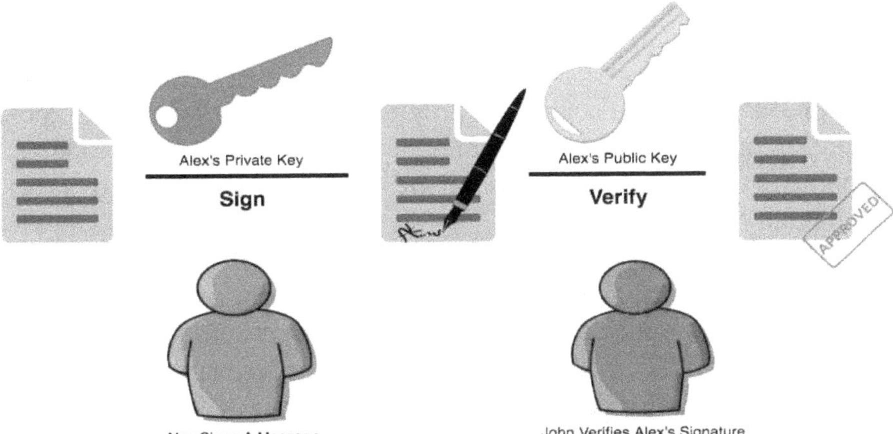

Digital signatures play an important role in cryptocurrency systems, because they prove ownership of funds and allow the individual in control of those funds to spend them.

For example, the digital signature algorithm that is utilized in Bitcoin is known as the **Elliptic Curve Digital Signature Algorithm**, which is also known as ECDSA. ECDSA is the algorithm that underpins the signature scheme in Bitcoin, and it is based on elliptic curve cryptography. This is the same cryptographic approach that is used in producing private and public key pairs. In Bitcoin, a digital signature is effectively intended to serve three distinct purposes:

Firstly, a digital signature serves as proof that the owner of a private key, who will by extension have ownership of his/her funds, has indeed authorized that those funds can be spent.

Secondly, a digital signature serves as proof that the authorization is undeniable.

Thirdly, a digital signature proves that the transaction that has been authorized by the signature has not or cannot be modified by anyone after it has been signed.

What are the benefits of Blockchains over Traditional Finance?

Trustless: The blockchain is immutable and automates trusted transactions between counterparties who do not need to know each other. Transactions are only executed when programmed conditions are met by both parties.

Unstoppable: Once the conditions programmed into a blockchain protocol are met, an initiated transaction cannot be undone, changed, or stopped. It's going to execute and nothing – no bank, government, or third party – can stop it.

Immutable: Records on a blockchain cannot be changed or tampered with – Bitcoin has never been hacked. A new block of transactions is only added after a complex mathematical problem is solved and verified by a consensus mechanism. Each new block has a unique cryptographic key resulting from the previous block's information and key being added into a formula.

Decentralized: No single entity maintains the network. Unlike centralized banks, decisions on the blockchain are made via consensus. Decentralization is essential because it ensures people can easily access and build on the platform, and there are multiple points of failure.

Lower Cost: In the traditional finance system, you pay third parties like banks to process transactions. The blockchain eliminates these intermediaries and reduces fees, with some systems returning fees to miners and stakers.

Peer-to-Peer: Cryptocurrencies like Bitcoin, let you send money directly to anyone, anywhere in the world, without an intermediary like a bank charging transaction or handling fees.

Transparent: Public blockchains are open-source software, so anyone can access them to view transactions and their source code. They can even use the code to build new applications and suggest improvements to the code. Suggestions are accepted or rejected via consensus.

Universal Banking: 2 billion people globally do not have a bank account. Because anyone can access the blockchain to store money, it's a great way to bank the unbanked and protect against theft that can happen due to holding cash in physical locations.

What are the Disadvantages of Blockchains?

Public open source blockchains are not without their hazards and challenges. Here is a list of the top concerns:

1. **Environmental Impact**

Blockchain networks like Bitcoin use a lot of electricity to validate transactions, leading to environmental concerns. For example, Bitcoin consumes more electricity than a small, medium-sized European country, and Bitcoin mining was threatening China's climate change goals in past years.

However, many would argue that Bitcoin is held to higher environmental standards than anyone and anything. This may be true, especially if you consider that the blockchain and Bitcoin are an alternative to the traditional finance system that uses much more electricity and has a much larger environmental impact.

A study by Galaxy Digital suggests Bitcoin energy consumption is less than half that of the traditional banking system. If anything, you could argue that Bitcoin is a step in the right direction for the environment.

No one Is saying that making strides to lowering the carbon footprint shouldn't be on the agenda (this is already happening with some mining farms shifting to renewable energy sources like solar panels and the El Salvadoran President calling for a plan to use geothermal energy (volcanoes) to mine Bitcoin).

But it's crucial to maintain a balanced view when viewing the cost, environmental impact, and blockchain benefits. The good news is most of the existing Blockchain are moving to Proof of Stake in which environmental impact is never an issue at all!

2. Personal Responsibility

One of blockchains and cryptocurrencies' most significant advantages is also its biggest weakness. When you invest in public open-source blockchains by mining or buying cryptocurrencies and store it in your cryptocurrency wallet (your wallet is like your bank account, except only you can access it and have the passwords), only you control your money.

You are your own bank— and this is great! But if you lose your seed phrases – the list of words that give you access to recover your wallets – there is no recourse (compared to banks where you can reset your password). Your money is lost forever.

Unsurprisingly, a large portion of Bitcoin remains permanently lost. According to some estimates, 20% or 3.7 million of the currently minted Bitcoin is probably lost forever.

3. Growing Pains

Even though public blockchains remain more efficient than traditional banking systems, decentralization comes at the cost of scalability. Trying to grow blockchain networks to global capacity, in turn, is the root cause of speed inefficiencies. It's why, as we saw, Bitcoin and Ethereum can only process a maximum of seven and 30 transactions, respectively, compared to Visa's 24,000.

Luckily solutions are being built to improve scalability and the speed of transactions. For example, the lightning network allows transactions to happen off the Bitcoin blockchain to speed up transactions. On Ethereum, many innovative Layer 2 (L2) solutions are being developed to improve scalability and speed including rollups, zero-knowledge proofs and side chains. But still good that you can send money from your comfort zone to any corner of the world within few minutes with blockchain.

4. False Narratives

Some cryptocurrencies are undoubtedly used in unlawful activity. The most famous example is **Silk Road**: people laundered money and bought drugs on the platform using Bitcoin.

However, this is no different from the illegal activity that constantly happens when people use other currencies like the Dollar.

This false narrative that cryptocurrencies are only or mainly used for illicit activities only delays their inevitable adoption, which can hugely benefit everyone, including the financial system.

Promising Blockchain Use Cases and Killer Applications

Blockchain technology is currently used across various industries like supply chain, healthcare, retail, media and advertising, financial services, insurance, travel and transportation, oil and gas, and gaming.

Here are some promising use cases:

- **Cryptocurrencies**: The 'killer app' of blockchains today is internet money. Cryptocurrencies let you transfer value faster and cheaper across borders without a bank. Besides Bitcoin and Ethereum, other digital currency examples include Polkadot (DOT), NEO, Cardano (ADA), Tether (USDT), Binance Coin (BNB), and Litecoin (LTC).

- **Smart Contracts**: These blockchain applications are contracts that automatically execute without an intermediary once condition written into the computer code are met.

- **Decentralized Banking**: The use of blockchain technology is also proliferating in banking. For example, many banks like Barclays, Canadian Imperial Bank, and UBS are interested in how blockchain can make their back-office settlement systems more efficient.

- **Central bank digital currencies (CBDCs):** are the digital form of a government-issued currency that isn't pegged to a physical commodity. They are issued by central banks, whose role is to support financial services for a nation's government and its commercial-banking system, set monetary policy, and issue currency. Nine banks including State Bank of India, Bank of Baroda, Union Bank of India, HDFC Bank, ICICI Bank, Kotak Mahindra Bank, Yes Bank, IDFC First Bank, and HSBC have been participating in the pilot of CBDC-Wholesale as of June 2023. Countries like Australia, china and India are piloting both use cases for their CBDCs.

- **Video Games/Art**: You may have heard Crypto Kitties—a game launched on the Ethereum blockchain. One of the virtual pets in the game was sold for over $100,000.

- **Peer-to-peer Energy Trading**: People buy or sell energy directly without an intermediary.

- **Supply chain and logistics tracking**: Blockchain is being used to track precious metals' origins and foods. For example, Walmart and IBM worked together to create a food traceability system based on open-source ledger technology, making it easier to trace contaminated food.

- **Healthcare process optimization**: Blockchain can speed up the time required to pay health insurance payments to patients and store and securely share medical data and records.

- **Real estate processing platform**: Property ownership records can be securely stored and verified on the blockchain. These records cannot be tampered with, so you can trust they're accurate and more easily verify property ownership.

- **NFT marketplaces**: These are marketplaces that allow you to buy nonfungible tokens (NFTs): digital tokens of things like paintings and clothing.

- **Music royalties tracking:** Blockchain can trace music streams and immediately pay those who contributed to a song.

- **Anti-money laundering tracking system:** Authorities can more easily track the original source of money because every transaction on the blockchain is recorded and leaves behind a tamper-proof trail.

- **Personal identity security**: Traditional systems for storing identities are insecure and fragmented. Blockchain provides a unified, immutable, and interoperable infrastructure so you can store and manage records securely and efficiently.

- **New insurance distribution methods**: For example, peer-to-peer insurance, parametric insurance, and microinsurance.

- **Automated Advertising Campaigns:** Advertisers can use smart contracts to automate advertising campaigns, e.g., an audience is only shown an ad when specific criteria are met.

How can businesses benefit from Blockchain?

Let's look at the business-specific advantages of blockchain technology.

- As mentioned above, the blockchain is a great way to build trust among entities that have never worked together. As such, it is an excellent way for businesses to work together without requiring a trusted third party.
- The blockchain can help create a consortium of businesses and provide an operational structure with no central "leader." This can allow multiple businesses to interact effectively and share information.

- The fact that all data stored within blockchains are immutable has game-changing security implications. It's no longer possible for malicious centralized parties to tamper with crucial data.

- By removing the need for trusted third parties, the overall organizational costs go down significantly. Plus, taking away these intermediaries drastically increases operational speeds. For example, Walmart used blockchain to trace the source of sliced mangoes in seconds. Normally, this process would take a week.

- The blockchain is a major boon for companies that rely on or operate supply chains. The blockchain's transparency helps fix a majority of the issues present in traditional supply chain structures. For example, not only has Walmart successfully applied blockchain in their supply chain via IBM, but the medical industry is actively using the tech in their crackdown on counterfeit medication.

Blockchain is the Present and the Future

With many promising real-world use cases like faster cross-border payments and smart contracts, blockchain technology is here to stay.

As more companies realize how the blockchain can help them, they'll commit more resources, money, and time into the technology—and even more use cases will emerge. While we understand that blockchain technology will remain a complex topic for many, it really doesn't have to be for you.

Part Two:

Ways of investing in Cryptocurrency

When you think of investing in cryptocurrency, you might think about buying and holding one or more crypto coins. Buying cryptocurrency directly is probably the most common way to add crypto exposure to your portfolio, but when it comes to investing in cryptocurrency, you have more different options.

One of the biggest challenges for investors is not getting caught up in the hype. Digital currencies have quickly risen to prominence in the portfolios of many retail and institutional investors. At the same time, analysts have continued to caution investors about the volatile nature and unpredictability of cryptocurrencies. However, instead of exposing yourself to the volatility of crypto, you can make money by investing in it passively or in other ways.

In this article, we will explore the different options for cryptocurrency investments and help you choose the one that suits you best.

I. HODL

What is HODL?

HODL refers to a **long-term strategy** for investing in cryptocurrencies. An investor purchase and hold the cryptocurrency for an extended period ignoring complex price fluctuations in the cryptocurrency market and focusing on long-term price appreciation. Furthermore, it is also an acronym for **"Hold on for Dear Life."**

Its propagation is linked to a famous typo that emerged in a post on a bitcoin forum called bitcointalk.org in 2013. The post was "I AM HODLING," actually intending "I AM HOLDING." It became a buzzword, and since then, the term has been widely used in the **bitcoin** and **cryptocurrency** world to mention holding.

Key Takeaways

- HODL is a crypto lingo indicating the investment strategy of buying and holding an asset for an extended period to gain from its long-term price appreciation.
- For amateurs in the crypto market, holding assets for an extended period saves them from the complications of other strategies timing the market like day trading, swing trading, or high-frequency trading.
- The buy and hold strategy may possess the risk of not having a centralized agency of control and uncertainty in the future of cryptocurrencies. Moreover, it does not utilize the benefits of high volatile nature of cryptocurrency.

HODLING as a Strategy and Guiding Philosophy

HODL, as an acronym for "hold on for dear life," has become a mantra among crypto enthusiasts denoting a long-term approach to cryptocurrency investing. This approach mirrors GameKyuubi's rationale in the original post that novice traders are likely to botch their attempts to time the market, and should simply hold their coin.

For cryptocurrency maximalists, HODL represents more than a strategy for reigning in **FOMO** (Fear of Missing Out), **FUD** (Fear, Uncertainty, and Doubt), and other profit-eroding emotions. Long-term crypto HODLers stay invested because they believe that cryptocurrencies will eventually replace government-issued fiat currencies as the basis of all economic structures. Should that occur, then the exchange rates between cryptocurrencies and fiat money would become irrelevant to crypto holders.

Predictably, a meme best captures this HODL maximalist philosophy. Neo from *The Matrix* asks Morpheus, "What are you trying to tell me, that I can trade my Bitcoin for millions someday?" Morpheus responds, "No Neo, I'm trying to tell you that when you're ready … you won't have to."

When to HODL?

Based on these principles, the best time to HODL is now, always, and forever. A true believer would always hold on to their tokens, even if markets crash or become extremely volatile. HODLing becomes an ideological belief about the long-term prospects of blockchain technology, cryptocurrencies, and the communities that have formed around them.

How Does HODL in Cryptocurrency Work?

HODL has been a famous slang word among investors in the blockchain community since 2013. Whenever the crypto value plunges to the bottom, the term "hodling" is used by many to indicate that they will hold on to the crypto purchases without selling it for a lengthy period riding the trajectory with the hope that price will appreciate significantly.

The hodling or holding strategy of making money by awaiting a longer period is opposite to the "time the market" concept where investors buy and sell short term. Market sentiments do not sway hodlers, and they don't panic by hearing news that might affect the cryptocurrency value. However, they may buy more if the price drops. Furthermore, they usually avoid third-party services for safeguarding their assets. The hodling strategy is very similar to the buy and holds **investing strategy** used for stocks, and the term 'hodl stock' indicates not to sell the stocks influenced by frequent swings.

Cryptocurrencies such as bitcoin have been volatile in the short term, but the long-term trend indicates the value has increased. For example, the **bitcoin valued** below 10,000 USD in 2019, revolves around a level above 40,000 USD in 2021, around 24,000 USD in 2022 and around 30,000 in the middle of 2023. One can buy bitcoin and then wait for years then sell it for a profit. It's not unheard of for people to double or even triple their invested amounts. Generally, people who are more patient and invest large sums of money are more likely to gain huge profits.

Is HODL Strategy Safe?

Numerous things add to the risk associated with the HODL strategy and cryptocurrency. Even though it attracts many fancy investors, it is still a new and highly volatile concept. The absence of a central authority to control the crypto operations, the absence of worldwide acceptance as a **medium of exchange**, and uncertainty in the future make it unsafe compared to strategies utilizing the frequent swings and other conventional investments. Hence holding for the long term may put investors in danger.

Other Crypto Slang Terms

The crypto community has adopted several acronyms and terms (often with accompanying emojis) in addition to HODLing. Many of these also overlap with terms used in meme stock communities and forums. Some of these include:

- **FUD** (fear, uncertainty, doubt): Misinformation, negative headlines, and dire predictions about crypto, which should be ignored by true adherents.

- **FOMO** (fear of missing out): People jumping onto bandwagon trades or buying into bubbles rather than regretting missing the next big thing

- **Diamond Hands** 💎 🤲: Exhibiting extreme fortitude in HODLing, even as markets crash

- **Hold the line**: A battle cry to encourage others to stand firm with diamond hands in the face of volatility.

- **Paper hands** 🧻 🤲: This is a derogatory slur leveled against those who fail to maintain diamond hands. These are perceived as weak individuals without conviction who sell their crypto too quickly.

- **Mooning** 🚀 🌙: The idea that a crypto will rise extraordinarily high, as if to the moon.

- **Apes** 🦍: Members of the crypto or NFT community. Some have attributed this to a meme related to the movie Rise of the Planet of the Apes, but others have suggested that the label comes from the banding together of "dumb apes" to take on the Wall Street elite.

- **BTFD** (buy the f***ing dip): Buying the dips means going long on a stock after its price has declined in the near term and is meant to be repeated after each such drawdown.

Can you HODL Stocks?

While HODLing is generally associated with cryptocurrency investors, the buy-and-hold investing strategy that it represents is not limited to crypto investing.

Many stock investors "HODL" their investments for long periods of time, although stock prices are almost always less volatile than the prices of crypto assets. Investors in stocks who buy and hold can benefit from long-term price appreciation while experiencing much less price volatility than is associated with cryptocurrencies.

The HODL Coin

HODL may also refer to a DeFI token on the Binance Smart Chain (BSC). **HODL Coin (SHODL)** was launched in May 2021. Much like the term itself, HODL encourages users to hold onto their tokens for rewards in the Binance coin (BNB) that are distributed every three days. The rewards are generated from taxes collected on transactions made by users, such as sale, purchase, or transfer of HODL tokens. The tax amount is converted into BNB tokens and a percentage of the gains is redistributed back to users from the collective liquidity pool.

Pros

Using HODL has several benefits that make it ideal for amateurs to trust cryptocurrency investment. First, beginners only need to buy the cryptocurrency, which means investing and waiting for an extended period to gain long-term value appreciation. It is one of the simplest ways of trading bitcoin. In addition, it saves them from the risk of engaging in crypto **day trading**, **swing trading**, or **high-frequency trading**.

Short-term investing strategies might make money faster but at the cost of a steep learning curve. Before attempting other complex strategies, one must learn all the different elements influencing cryptocurrency and technical information. By using the HODL method, one can still make money from cryptocurrency while slowly learning about the other aspects of trading.

Cons

The most significant disadvantage of HODL is the amount of time needed to make the profit that an investor desires. In addition, the holding strategy makes the investors miss the opportunities to benefit from **short-term price fluctuations** in the crypto market.

The time required depends on how much an investor aims to make in the first place. For example, if they are looking to make a profit of 2%, it will probably take a short time to reach this goal. However, the main point of involving oneself in cryptocurrency is taking advantage of the significant short-term changes in the value of the crypto invested. Using HODL to double the deposit, for instance, is not uncommon. However, this might demand significantly more patience if the bitcoin value reduces considerably after buying it. The investor has to wait for an extended period locking his capital and experiencing too many swings. He should have enough capital capacity to stay away from selling low.

Do you know? When you bought $10 worth of Bitcoin for $0.0009 in 2009 you would be a multimillionaire with around $300,000,000 worth of bitcoins at this time of writing this book! Imagine that by just holding $10 for a decade to become multimillionaire! So, Holding can be one of the great strategies.

II. Trading

Trading is one of the most common and important ways of investing in cryptocurrency.

Trading is a fundamental economic concept that involves buying and selling assets. These can be goods and services, where the buyer pays the compensation to the seller. In other cases, the transaction can involve the exchange of goods and services between the trading parties.

In the context of the financial markets, the assets being traded are called financial instruments. These can be stocks, bonds, currency pairs on the Forex market, options, futures, margin products, cryptocurrency, and many others.

The term trading is commonly used to refer to short-term trading, where traders actively enter and exit positions over relatively short time frames. However, this is a slightly misleading assumption. In fact, trading may refer to a wide range of different strategies, such as day trading, swing trading, trend trading, and many others.

What is investing?

Investing is allocating resources (such as capital) with the expectation of generating a profit. This can include using money to fund and kickstart a business or buying land with the goal of reselling it later at a higher price. In the financial markets, this typically involves investing in financial instruments with the hopes of selling them later at a higher price.

The expectation of a return is core to the concept of investment (this is also known as **ROI**). As opposed to trading, investing typically takes a longer-term approach to wealth accrual. The goal of an investor is to build wealth over a long period of time (years, or even decades). There are plenty of ways to do that, but investors will typically use fundamental factors to find potentially good investment opportunities.

Due to the long-term nature of their approach, investors usually don't concern themselves with short-term price fluctuations. As such, they will typically stay relatively passive, without worrying too much about short-term losses.

Trading vs. investing – what's the difference?

Both traders and investors seek to generate profits in the financial markets. Their methods to achieve this goal, however, are quite different.

Generally, investors seek to generate a return over a longer period of time – think years or even decades. In this case you can call it **Holding/Hodling** because they use similar strategies. Since investors have a larger time horizon, their targeted returns for each investment tend to be larger as well.

Traders, on the other hand, try to take advantage of the market volatility. They enter and exit positions more frequently, and may seek smaller returns with each trade (since they're often entering multiple trades).

Which one is better?

Which one is more suitable for you? That's for you to decide. You can start educating yourself about the markets, and then learn by doing. Over time, you'll be able to determine which one suits better your financial goals, personality, and trading profile.

Getting Started with Cryptocurrency Trading

To get started with cryptocurrency trading, you'll need to choose a reputable cryptocurrency exchange like Binance trading platform and create an account. You should also do your research and educate yourself on the different cryptocurrencies available for trading. It's important to start with a small amount of capital and to only invest what you can afford to lose.

Once you've created an account and deposited funds, you can start trading. You can choose to buy and hold a cryptocurrency for a long-term investment, or you can actively trade it by buying and selling frequently. Remember to keep an eye on market volatility, liquidity, and security when trading cryptocurrencies.

Advantages of Crypto Trading

1. Easy Set up

You don't need to go through complex processes to start cryptocurrencies trading. The first requirement to start trading is a **mobile phone** and an **internet connection**. You must then open an account with a reliable crypto exchange or broker. So, if you're turning this into your career, you should only use the safest crypto exchanges.

It's also easy to open accounts on these exchanges. Furthermore, many exchanges require low minimum account balances. So, you likely won't have issues with funding your account.

Once you have an account and have funded your wallet, you're now ready to day trade cryptocurrencies.

And contrary to how it works for many businesses, you don't have to rent an office or worry about strategies to draw customers. Cryptocurrency trading like *day trading strategies* allows you to trade from your home or anywhere you find comfortable.

However, just like any business, you'll have to put in hard work studying the factors affecting the cryptos you want to trade and the price movement in search of trade entries. After all, there's no such thing as easy money.

2. 24/7 Accessibility

Since cryptocurrency isn't based on any traditional market, like forex or stock exchanges, you can trade crypto 24 hours a day. Because of this, you can schedule your day trading activities to the best time you want, either during the day, at night, or even during weekends.

The 24-hour accessibility gives global access to the crypto market, and you can trade cryptocurrency no matter your time zone. All you have to do is *plan your time* properly to make it work.

3. Benefit from Bull and Bear Markets

Crypto spot trading allows you to benefit from higher crypto prices. When you buy a crypto asset, your investment will increase as the asset's price rises. However, it will also lose value if the crypto's price falls

But if you take advantage of crypto derivatives, you can benefit from both a rising market and falling crypto prices. When you think the price of an asset is about to drop, it's possible to short an asset so you could make money even if the market falls. However, note that shorting anything could also lead to unlimited losses, as evidenced by the GameStop meme stock event in 2021.

4. Many Crypto Assets

When trading cryptocurrencies, you can access a wide range of assets. Many exchanges provide access to hundreds of cryptos, allowing traders to choose the ones that best fit their preferences from numerous options. For instance, Binance offers over 350 cryptocurrencies, while Coinbase and Bybit each have more than 250 cryptocurrencies for trading.

With this massive number of coins, you can easily diversify your portfolio, benefit from multiple cryptocurrencies simultaneously, and even help protect your income if some fail.

5. Diverse Trading Strategies

If you play to trade professionally, you should have a crypto trading strategy. Many day traders use scalping and day trading strategies to profit from the market since most trades carried out using them are closed within the same day.

These day trading strategies allow trading with different styles, like studying candlesticks to get market information and finding valuable patterns like the breakout and retest and the head and shoulders pattern. You can also use indicators and tools to get market data and combine all these with other analysis methods to make trading decisions.

You see your results faster with day trading strategies since most trades are concluded quickly. Cryptocurrency trading also allows you to trade with trading bots, which helps you to trade without your involvement. In this case, the bot handles a part of or the whole trading activity, and you only have to wait for the result.

6. Take Advantage of Market Volatility

Cryptocurrency volatility refers to the degree of crypto assets' price fluctuation over time. The crypto market is very volatile and experiences many short-term wild swings.

As much as fast intraday price movement can work against you if you do not manage risks well, it also presents many opportunities you can exploit. The higher the volatility of an asset, the greater the chances of getting trading opportunities quickly.

7. Won't have to answer to a Boss

Being employed means you are subject to some rules and regulations, and they may limit your freedom. However, crypto day trading allows you to work at your own pace. This may be attractive if you value your independence and want more control over your work life.

Crypto trading also gives you total control over your investment decisions. You can choose which crypto to buy and sell and when you want to do it. This way, you take responsibility for your success or failure rather than rely on others.

8. You Can Use Leverage

Leverages are funds that exchanges or brokers make available to traders to increase the size of their trading position beyond the size of their actual trading balance. With leverage, you have higher exposure to the market. Although this entails greater risk, you could also get more considerable gains if the trade goes in your favor.

For example, with a trading balance of $10,000, a 10% profit would give you $1,000 as profit. However, if you use a leverage of 1:20, you can open trades worth as much as $200,000 while having the same $10,000 as your trading balance. With the same leverage, a 10% increase would give you a profit of $20,000.

However, it's important to note that there are also some risks associated with trading cryptocurrencies. Some of the most notable risks include:

- **Volatility**: Cryptocurrencies are known for their volatility, which means that their prices can fluctuate wildly. This can make it difficult to predict the future price of a cryptocurrency and can lead to losses.

- **Hacking**: Cryptocurrencies are often stored in digital wallets, which can be hacked. If your wallet is hacked, you could lose all of your cryptocurrency.

- **Regulation**: The cryptocurrency market is still largely unregulated, which means that there is no one to protect you if you are scammed or if your cryptocurrency is stolen. So be wise while choosing a crypto and an exchange platform.

√ Crypto Trading Can Be Lucrative, But It Isn't for Everyone

Note: crypto trading like *day trading* provides a lot of attractive advantages. Thus, those who can take the time and effort to learn the required skills, be abreast of market trends, and master the psychology of trading can make a lot for themselves.

III. Becoming a crypto Miner or Validator

This is also a great way to get involved in cryptocurrency investments, but it requires some initial investment. We'll go over how to do it step-by-step.

1. Cryptocurrency Mining?

Cryptocurrency mining is the process by which blockchain networks create new coins. Mining only works with ***PoW blockchains***, which use different types of algorithms. The Bitcoin network for instance relies on the ***SHA-256*** algorithm, while Ethereum was using the ***Ethash algorithm.***

Mining investment is a very lucrative business if you have some initial money. Before you decide on mining you need to find out about the mining algorithm as this points to the type of hardware supported on the network. While some cryptocurrencies allow for use of specialised mining equipment called *ASICs*, others are ASIC-resistant, making it possible to mine with a graphics card. I will highlight more on this in one of the sections below.

Anyone can become a miner as long as they have the right mining equipment or the computational power needed to mine a new block on the network.

In mining, special computers, also called **miners** or **nodes**, compete to solve difficult mathematical problems seeking out a value that identifies the valid block. The value is a hash (calculation) called a *nonce* and how long it takes to get one depends on the protocol. Bitcoin takes about 10 minutes, while Ethereum takes about 15 seconds and Ravencoin has a 1-minute block generation time.

Once a miner is the first to find the value, they broadcast it to the network. The decentralised nature of the process requires that a majority of miners verify the block before it is added to the blockchain. The winning miner gets a block reward that releases new cryptocurrency coins into circulation.

Why cryptocurrency Miners are important?

From the above section, it is clear that miners play a big role in any PoW blockchain network. It's not just verifying transactions; their role goes a long way in ensuring the network remains safe and active at all times.

How do miners do this?

When verifying transactions, they do due diligence by ascertaining that no block can be added to the blockchain twice. In short, they solve the **double-spending** problem. Double spending means the expenditure of the same digital currency twice or more to avail the multiple services. It is a technical flaw that allows users to duplicate money.

Blockchains make it much easier to prevent this problem. The technology underlying cryptocurrency timestamps each group of transactions before broadcasting them to nodes. Each block also has a hash that contains a timestamp of the previous block, making it difficult for the nodes to send a transaction twice.

To guarantee a higher degree of security, miners verify and validate the transactions before they are formally regarded as part of the continuously growing blockchain.

Miners also secure the network by dedicating their computational power to the blockchain. Note that the number of people (miners) on a network is also essential to its security. In particular, when the number of miners increases, the network enjoys a higher **hashrate**. A higher network hashrate implies there are adequate active decision-makers who can avert any security risk on the network.

Cryptocurrency Mining Limitations

As noted above, all Proof of Work networks use miners to process transactions and to secure the network. However, different networks approach this critical component differently, with certain limitations in place which you might need to keep in mind before you decide to mine a given coin.

The first limitation is about coin supply and how these coins are released into circulation through mining.

Some coins have a **hard cap supply**, which means there's a fixed number of coins that will ever exist. For instance, Bitcoin has a fixed supply of 21 million BTC, which is also copied by many Bitcoin forks. Litecoin is fixed at 84 million; while Ethereum Classic is set to have a fixed supply of 210,700,000 ETC. Others like Electroneum and Ravencoin have limited their total supply to 21 billion coins.

Since some miners can use superior mining devices to earn maximum returns, the capping of coin supply and the halving of block rewards are also designed to create mining difficulty. This means coin supply remains limited despite the efficiency of mining machines and the number of people joining the network.

Tip to mine cryptocurrencies efficiently for greater profit

You can make a profit mining crypto without investing in expensive mining machines or having to assemble large mining rigs just to get a higher count of hashing power. The best way to make a significant profit from mining is to identify a coin that allows you to mine via a **mining pool**. You then identify a pool with the lowest fees, or no fees at all, and whose operations are in a region with the lowest electricity costs. This way, your hashrate will attract less cost on power and you won't pay a percentage every time you receive a share of the reward.

Technical aspects of Mining Cryptocurrency

I am going to explain the more technical aspects of crypto mining in this section. Some of the key terms we shall focus on are hashrate and processing power. I shall also help you understand the essence of having a higher hashrate and the resources you need to mine profitably.

What does hashrate mean?

Hashrate is a measure of the amount of computing power needed to mine a new block of transactions and earn a block reward. It tells you how fast a mining machine can work towards solving a new coin. The machines make several guesses every second, with each calculation called a hash. The hashrate of your computer or mining hardware lets you know how efficient a given CPU, GPU, or ASIC miner, is at completing tasks.

You can also add up individual computing power contributions of miners to measure the total computing power of all participants on a cryptocurrency network. The higher the hashrate the better it is for the network.

Why is a higher hashrate important?

A mining rig with a higher hashrate packs more hashing power, which means it can mine more quickly and efficiently compared to a machine with a low count.

A higher hashrate of the entire network shows that more miners are active, which has a role in the increase in mining difficulty and thus mining competition. However, the most critical aspect of a higher network hashrate is that more miners equate to better decentralization. In return, there is better network protection against a **51% attack.**

The higher hashrate makes it difficult and highly unprofitable for bad actors to hijack the system, thereby enhancing the network's security.

How is hashrate measured?

Hashrate is measured in hashes per second or solutions per second (H/s or Sol/s) on different networks. But what this means is that you are looking at how many calculations you get per second with the hardware you have.

The five common units for measuring this are kilohashes per second (Kh/s), megahashes per second (Mh/s), gigahashes per second (Gh/s), terahashes per second (Th/s), and petahashes per second (Ph/s).

Kilo means 1000 hashes and the number increases to 1 million, 1 billion, 1 trillion, and 1 quadrillion hashes for each of the other four ratings.

When choosing a device for mining, you should consider its hashrate. A machine with the required hashing power increases your chances of making profits.

Processing Power: CPU & GPU

When it comes to mining cryptocurrencies, processing power refers to the speed of the mining machine. It is how fast the computer's microprocessor calculates the maths that leads to finding new blocks and hence block rewards.

The faster, and hence more powerful the processor, the better your chances of finding a new block when competing against other miners. It may be the reason why you might mine some cryptocurrencies with the central processing unit (CPU) power but not others. For those that you can't, you probably need a faster processor called the graphics processing unit (GPU).

You could comfortably mine Bitcoin using CPU in the early days, but that is now obsolete and the same goes for CPU mining on most other major networks. The simple explanation for this is that the CPU suits simple math calculations. The alternative is GPU mining, which offers more hashing power and is suitable for complex mathematical calculations.

Today, most miners use GPU mining and application-specific integrated circuits (ASICs), but there was another piece of equipment specifically tailored for crypto mining.

The **field-programmable gate array (FPGA)** is a mining machine that was designed by miners seeking higher processing speeds but at low power consumption. These customized fixed-function devices are however not common as miners go for GPUs and ASICs.

The ASIC is specifically designed to mine a particular PoW algorithm, with many available for SHA-256. However, other than being expensive, they are not easily accessible to individual miners as manufacturers and vendors prefer large orders.

Hashrate needed to mine cryptocurrency profitably

As you might already have noticed, mining different coins require different levels of hashrate. The difference arises from the fact that network difficulty is not the same. At the same time, the hashrate and difficulty are not static, meaning requirements fluctuate from time to time.

Also importantly, miners have to follow different consensus rules. The type of hardware also matters, depending on whether the protocol is ASIC-resistant or not.

Overall, you need a decent machine that gives you enough hashrate to mine individually or to get a good share reward from a pool.

Below is an example of a network difficulty chart for Bitcoin, illustrating the adjustments as hashrate increases.

Bitcoin mining difficulty

Pros
- You earn a reward when you create a new block.
- By participating in the verification of transactions, you keep the decentralised platform active 24/7.
- You earn massive sums if you use machines with high hashing power and manage the power cost.
- You can sell mining hardware if you no longer use them.
- You help to protect the network from 51% attack and double payment problems.

Cons

- Mining is energy-intensive and needs huge amounts of electricity.
- Crypto remains volatile, which exposes you to the risk of making a loss.

Mining - How to get started

In this section, I will cover what you should do to get started with cryptocurrency mining. Some of the key areas we will focus on are the best hardware and software and the costs you should be prepared to incur.

Best Mining Hardware for Cryptocurrency

As we have mentioned before, you need cost-effective hardware to mine cryptocurrencies. Different cryptocurrencies use different mining algorithms and that too reflects in the mining hardware.

For Bitcoin and some select coins, ASIC miners are the best as they offer the highest power and are efficient. However, cost is a key deterrent for new miners seeking to start operations.

For example, not many can afford the new **Bitmain Antminer S19 Pro** that packs 110 TH/s, and power consumption of 3250W. This ASIC beast sells at over $18,000 when included with a power supply unit (PSU) and power cords. That's too expensive, but it's the best hardware for mining Bitcoin's SHA-256 algorithm.

When it comes to ASIC –resistant networks, you can only efficiently mine using GPU hardware. Nvidia and AMD graphics cards are the best for mining crypto and are usually used to assemble mining rigs to get the desired range of computational power.

For example, Nicehash offers a customised 10x NVIDIA RTX 3060 Ti mining rig that punches a decent 600 MH/s with only 1400W. A single RTX 3060 goes for about $399.

As you choose a coin to start mining, the first step is to find out what it costs to acquire the hardware.

Other costs to be considered

While hardware is considered the most important mining component, you can't achieve anything without enough power supply. Devices that use more power are more profitable, which means higher costs on electricity and high-end PSUs.

You also need to consider how much you will pay for electricity, both for running the mining machines and the elaborate cooling system. Note that

ASICs may have fans, but you might need to install extra fans for better results, including when you assemble a mining rig.

The best way to cushion against the extra costs is to use cheap electricity and use miners with the highest efficiency possible.

Start Mining!

Once you have the hardware set up, you are a step away from mining cryptocurrency. The next step is to **download compatible mining software.**

If you are a Windows user, download a Windows-supported software miner, likewise for Linux and Mac. You could also mine some coins using your Android mobile phone, which then calls for mobile-supported software.

I have also mentioned that you might need to join a **mining pool**. Select one and proceed to configure your mining software, connecting your hardware to the pool and the network you wish to mine. If you have the wallet set up, software configured, and hardware powered up- start mining.

Mining Solution/Services

Mining has become too complex on some networks that the best alternative for most people is to join mining pools. A mining service or provider makes it possible for many miners to combine hardware power and to mine cryptocurrency as a single unit with a significantly higher hashrate.

The most important tip when looking to join a mining pool is to ensure you choose the one that guarantees you a reward for your efforts.

One of the factors to consider is the **mining fees**. The average fee should be 1%. It is important to pay attention to this since you want to save on the costs to increase your earnings.

Server location is also important. When you choose a server that is closer to you, you increase the chances of creating more valid blocks. If the servers are located in a country where electricity is cheap, you have an added advantage in terms of cost reductions.

The mining pool must also be trustworthy. Established pools are often dependable. If you want to join a new pool, research widely to see what the mining community has to say about them.

Moreover, you should consider the payout scheme. Some are geared towards luck, while others even share rewards. Some come with high risks but reward their miners handsomely. So, it's a matter of your preference.

Other factors you should consider are the pool uptime, minimum payout and total pool hash power.

There are several mining pools to choose from, with top options depending on the coin you want to mine. In this case, do a little research for the coin in question and see which pools are the best for the cryptocurrency. Use the above points to guide you.

What if you want to mine cryptocurrency but don't want to buy hardware or run it yourself? The answer is to try cloud mining.

A cloud mining service allows you to rent hashrate and mine for a given period as agreed in a contract. It takes away the responsibility of acquiring and running mining machines, with added advantages being that you can mine any coin at a cost you are comfortable with.

However, cloud mining has its fair share of weaknesses that you should pay close attention to before buying the contracts. The prevalence of scams in this industry is worrying. If you fail to do due diligence, you are likely to fall prey to them.

Some cloud miners can also take advantage of your naivety to pay you less than you are worth. Others might terminate your contract as they will.

So, it's important to read all the clauses in your contract before giving your signature.

With that in mind, top cloud mining services on the market to check out include Genesis Mining, HashFlare, NiceHash, and Hashgains. You can also do some research on the specific coin to find which cloud mining service is supported.

Where can I save my coins after Mining?

Before you start mining any cryptocurrency, you need to choose the right crypto wallet. This is where you will receive your block rewards.

You have a lot of excellent options to choose from in the market. However, hardware wallets are the best if you want to securely store your coins. They offer the right balance between convenience and security.

A good wallet will help you keep your newly minted coins safe, but also allow you to send or trade with ease. I have already explained about crypto wallets in **Part One**.

2. Becoming Validator

Crypto Validators are new "payment processors" in decentralized networks, and as such, they produce blockchain rewards.

It sounds simple, doesn't it? However, the definition of validators in crypto is much more complex than that. Also, the role of a validator may change depending on the consensus mechanism each blockchain uses.

In this guide to validators in blockchain, we look closely at this entity and its indispensable role. Furthermore, we analyze four validator use cases in different blockchains and their benefits. Read on to discover how validators work and whether staking is profitable!

What are Validators in Blockchain?

A crypto validator is a participant in a blockchain responsible for verifying transactions. When it determines the accuracy of a transaction, the validator adds it to the distributed ledger. This way, the legitimacy of the blockchain and, subsequently, its transparent functioning remains intact. It's like Mining but with quite difference, for example mining is based on Proof of Work.

KYC and Audit Solutions for Every Project!

The easiest way to understand what role validators play is to go back to the blockchain definition.

Blockchain is a system functioning on a distributed register of information. A network of nodes(computers) supports this register by storing and running the same version of it simultaneously.
For example, a blockchain is like a book (register) with countless authors (nodes). Each of these authors can contribute to this book. However, before they do so, they must receive the validation of the other authors. That's when the other nodes, or their delegates, analyze the author's data. And if it is accurate, they validate it and add it to the register in a new block.

The necessary number of validators differs between blockchains. Also, the validation process may vary depending on the consensus mechanism of every blockchain. Ultimately, the chain can only contain accurate data that has received the entire community's validation.

In most blockchains, users receive rewards (block rewards) for taking up a validator role. This way, the system incentivizes its participants to continue the ledger's expansion process.
On the other hand, all blockchains use penalties for users who put up inaccurate data for validation. Generally, these participants receive a temporary or permanent ban from the system. That's one way the ledger ensures its protection against malicious use.

How many types of Crypto Validators are there?

The job of a blockchain validator may be relatively easy. You receive some data, check its accuracy, and validate it or not. However, validating new blocks on a distributed ledger is easier said than done.

Nevertheless, a validator on Bitcoin differs from a validator on Ethereum, which differs from one on Solana. So, what sets them apart? Let's find out!

Validators on Proof-of-Work Blockchains

Proof-of-work (PoW) blockchains require validators to show they "worked" on checking data before adding it to the chain. That's why validators get a more zeal-laden term, **miners**.
Bitcoin is the first PoW blockchain and the most popular one using this consensus mechanism. Miners use supercomputers, Application-Specific Integrated Circuit (ASIC) machines, to calculate data coming in as mathematical puzzles. Each computer is a Bitcoin node. The first miner to successfully validate a new data block receives a block reward.

Validators on Proof-of-Stake Blockchains

On Proof-of-Stake (PoS) blockchains, users have to stake a specific amount of the ledger's native token to become validators. Also, the system may randomly choose validators and reward those who participate correctly in the network.

Some of the most popular PoS blockchains include **Ethereum, Avalanche**, and **Solana**, among many others. These ledgers use Proof-of-Stake to incentivize users to lock up value within the network. This way, they ensure its fast progress and development.

Validators on Byzantine Fault Tolerance Blockchains

Blockchains that do not use PoW or PoS as consensus mechanisms can still employ validators. For instance, Stellar is a blockchain operating on the **Byzantine Fault Tolerance** consensus mechanism.

When a decentralized ledger uses this mechanism, some nodes can provide inaccurate data for validation. These nodes may be corrupt and intentionally misuse the network. However, as long as most validator nodes are honest, the validation process has an accuracy guarantee. As a result, it adds more data to the chain despite the malicious actions of some of its nodes.

On **Stellar**, the validation process predicts that some messages may corrupt. However, data can receive validation as long as these nefarious messages exceed one-third of the total. Otherwise, the transaction would become invalid.

How do Validators work on a Blockchain?

To become a validator on Proof-of-Stake blockchains, you have to stake (wager) your assets. What is staking?

Staking is a way to make your crypto holdings work for you and multiply. This happens through rewards you receive for committing your crypto to validate and confirm blockchain transactions. Below are the four most popular PoS networks that use this system. More on Staking later.

Validators on Ethereum (ETH)

While Ethereum started as a Proof-of-Work ledger, it slowly moved to a Proof-of-Stake (PoS) consensus mechanism. Once migration ends, participants to Ethereum turn into validators by staking no less than 32 ETH. This is already done in 2022 i.e Ethereum moved to PoS.
The system randomly chooses validators to create new blocks. They were responsible for checking and confirming blocks they don't make. The stake should incentivize the validator to provide accurate data and good behavior. Otherwise, it might lose a portion of its stakings.

How to Become a Validator on Ethereum

As of now, to validate blocks on Ethereum, you will need the following:

- Stake 32 ETH to become a total validator or some ETH to join a staking pool.
- Run an 'Eth1' or Mainnet client or a backend API.
- Batch transactions into a new block or check the work of other validators.

With these simple actions, you can support the chain running securely. Also, it would be best to refrain from malicious activities, going offline, or failing to validate. Otherwise, you will lose a significant portion of your stakings. In return for honest validating, you should receive up to 7.3% of your annual stakings.

Validators on Solana (SOL)

Solana is a high-throughput blockchain among some of the most recently successful crypto projects. Since its launch in early 2020, it has swiftly grown into the go-to platform for over 400 projects spanning DeFi, NFTs, Web3, and more.

Solana uses **Delegated-Proof-of-Stake** (DPoS) as a consensus mechanism. Anyone holding the platform's native token, SOL, can participate in the validating process. However, you can delegate your SOL to a validator which does your entire job. This means that you don't need a minimum amount to stake. You can have only 1 SOL and still be an active part of Solana as a delegator.

The validator receives stakes from delegators, which increases its chances for more slots and, subsequently, more rewards.

As a delegator, you can withdraw your stakings at any time. You can do so regardless of the validator's performance and without providing a reason.

How to become a Validator on Solana

On Solana, you can go beyond the Delegator role and become a Validator. First, however, you will have to meet more requirements.

One prerequisite is learning how Solana works. This blockchain operates in epochs, which may be between 2 and 3 days long. Also, every epoch consists of 420,000 blocks and a targeted block time of 400ms.

As a validator, you have to vote on every single block. So to earn rewards, you must take advantage of all of them. Even more, rewards represent a factor of the percentage success in voting and the stake you have relative to the rest of the network.

For example, if you hold 2% of the network's total stake and vote on every block, you earn 2% of the rewards. And to reach this performance, you will need the following:

- A powerful server running on a 12 cores / 24 threads CPU of 2.8GHZ or higher
- Pay for vote fees, which may amount to 1 SOL per day.
- Stake at least 5K SOL from your funds or 50K SOL from delegators.

IV. Passive income opportunities

1. Crypto Staking

While most crypto investors begin their journey by purchasing and trading coins on a centralized exchange, more advanced users and investors quickly learn that **crypto staking** is one of the most consistent methods of accumulating cryptocurrencies.

Crypto staking, often referred to simply as "**staking**", is a method of earning passive income using cryptocurrencies. Although it can be intimidating to dive into a new concept in crypto, staking is an essential piece of knowledge to fully understand your crypto investments and the potential to leverage them to generate passive gains over time.

At a high level, crypto staking uses your digital assets to earn returns (similar to interest or dividends) over time. Typically, these returns can outweigh those found in traditional finance. However, the returns are almost always denominated in highly volatile crypto assets, and there is risk involved to consider before locking up assets in a high-interest staking pool.

What exactly is Staking?

The act of staking most often refers to locking up a specific crypto asset to assist with running and validating the blockchain. As a reward for staking coins, there is a regular payment or reward given back to the users (referred to as "stakers"). There are other forms of staking associated with DeFi platform fee sharing, but this form of staking is not discussed here.

By committing tokens to stake, staked tokens are being used to ensure the validity of transactions. Since blockchains are decentralized, there needs to be a method of confirming the legitimacy of transactions. If there is no centralized authority to confirm the validity of each transaction, how do blockchains create a trustless ledger? While the exact approaches vary, each blockchain needs to use a "consensus mechanism" to validate and confirm transactions.

What are the Benefits of Staking?

By staking coins, investors are participating in the decentralized and trustless process that enables cryptocurrency blockchains to function. Of course, the benefits are not simply participating and learning more about the inner workings of blockchains. Rewards, typically paid in the blockchain's native token, are accumulated for each staker over time.

Long-term investors tend to favor staking tokens since the alternative is simply holding them in a wallet or on an exchange. By 'putting your money to work,' these assets are earning interest during the hold period.

How are Staking Rewards Calculated?

As investors consider staking, there will commonly be a rate of return (**APR** or **APY**) or reward percentage shown to give an estimate of the returns over time. These values give a sense of the expected rate of return; however, investors should investigate the **return time frame, lock-up periods, total token supply, reward plans** or **changes, auto-compounding**, and other **token-specific plans** that may influence returns. The best place to review is the blockchain's website for a whitepaper or discord group that can answer questions and provide clarity.

Keep in mind the fiat value of the token is not considered in most staking reward systems. While a stable or growing value token may offer extremely appealing rewards (token appreciation + staking rewards), the loss of value in fiat can easily wipe out any gains from staking. As with traditional finance, the largest promised returns often have a higher risk associated with them. A token with a large APY is probably more volatile in fiat value than a more established coin with moderate staking returns.

As of the writing of this article, the average rate of return on staking tokens is 9.6% annually with returns ranging from low-single-digits to 18%, 20%, or more depending on the type of token and the chain on which it is staked.

Risks of Staking

While staking can be an excellent way to build up a crypto portfolio, it is not without risks. As discussed briefly in this article, the primary staking risks are fiat value, lock-up or vesting periods, and counterparty risk with either the pool operator, the project team, or the chain itself.

Fiat Value

Any investor in crypto markets understands the volatile nature of these assets. Crypto prices in USD (or any native currency) can change at a rapid pace which may enhance or wipe out gains from staking. Even a 20% staking return can quickly evaporate in fiat value when the market shifts. On the other hand, upward price movements compound staking gains.

Lock-up Periods

Lock-ups or vesting is another consideration for an investor prior to choosing to stake tokens. For most coins, when you stake, you are committing to locking up your tokens for a set period of time. Sometimes, this is as short as a few hours, but is often a week, a month, or longer.

If you are actively seeking to trade or would like the freedom to react quickly to market conditions, then staking coins that require a lock-up may not be the best option. Keep in mind investment time frames. With compounding rewards and small, regular payments over time, staking is often a better choice for a long-term investor and a personal investment time frame is a key consideration.

Counterparty Risk

One additional risk consideration with cryptocurrency staking is called "counterparty risk." Counterparty risk is traditionally defined as the likelihood that the party with which you trust your assets may not uphold their side of the deal.

In terms of staking, if you are working through a staking pool that relies upon a pool operator to run the validator, there is a risk of fees or penalties assessed to the pool. These fees are typically assessed if the pool operator has downtime or dishonest actions.

How to Get Started

So now that you have a basic understanding of staking, the big question is "how do I get started?"

The process is not necessarily as complex or daunting as it may seem at first. Everyday users can get started with most large crypto exchanges (such as **Coinbase**) or on the respective project's website. Keep in mind that the process below is the simplest starting point. To become a full validator would require additional investment and technical knowledge beyond the scope of this article.

A quick overview of the simple process is as follows:

1. Determine the token to stake
2. Purchase tokens
3. Commit tokens to a staking pool

Let's walk through a quick example:

Determine the Token to Stake

As discussed previously, types of cryptocurrencies available to stake must use the Proof-of-Stake consensus mechanism. Additionally, we would like to compare fiat value over time, staking payout rates, and research the token as an investment.

There are analytics platform which are a great way to conduct this due diligence, using tools like analyzing various forms of staked Ether, such as Lido's stETH.

Purchase Tokens

This step is completed easily on your preferred crypto exchange. Popular cryptocurrency exchanges such as Coinbase are often set up to buy and stake in a few easy clicks. Depending on the token, you may be able to use a decentralized exchange such as **Uniswap.**

Keep in mind if you are purchasing the token outside of a centralized exchange, you will likely need a crypto wallet that supports the token. Popular crypto wallets vary depending on the coin, but links to reputable software wallets are commonly found on the official website of the project. Hardware wallets can be used for staking, but may need additional software such as Ledger.

Commit Tokens to a Staking Pool

Staking through a crypto exchange like Coinbase is as simple as selecting an option to "Buy & Stake" or after purchasing, going to the "Interest" section to commit tokens to staking. When using a centralized exchange, the process is simplified which comes at a cost of a reduced APR. Using an exchange may even help mitigate concerns around validator select and counterparty risk.

Other options may vary depending on where you purchase and hold your crypto. Wallets often offer staking and may require you to create a staking-specific account and then select a validator to join a staking pool. Be sure to investigate the validator prior to delegating tokens, to ensure you are reducing counterparty risk.

2. Lending

Crypto lending lets users borrow and lend cryptocurrencies for a fee or interest. You can instantly get a loan and start investing just by providing some collateral. This could be through a DeFi lending DApp or a cryptocurrency exchange. When your collateral falls below a certain value, you will need to top it up to the required level to avoid liquidation. When you return your loan plus a fee, your capital is unlocked.

You can also get collateral-free loans known as **flash loans**, which you must pay back within the same transaction. If you cannot do this, the lending transaction is reversed before it has the chance to be finalized. Crypto loans make borrowing and lending simple, and the process is completely automated by smart contracts. For many, it's an easy way to earn APY on crypto assets they HODL or access cheap credit.

However, just like any project, smart contract, or investment on the blockchain, crypto lending also involves financial risk. For example, if you use a volatile coin as collateral, you can be liquidated overnight. Smart contracts can also be hacked, attacked, or exploited, which often leads to big losses.

Before borrowing or lending, understand that you will lose custody of your coins. This removes them from your control and reduces your liquidity. Take note of all the terms and conditions of the loan to understand when you can access your funds and any fees involved.

When you think of gains and losses in crypto, volatile prices and hectic markets can come to mind. But that's not the only way to make money on the blockchain. Crypto lending is an easily-accessible service where you can lend out your funds with relatively low risk. On the other hand, you can also quickly gain access to borrowed digital assets at low-interest rates. Taking out and giving loans is often more straightforward, efficient, and cheap with crypto, making it an option worth exploring for both parties in a loan.

Crypto lending works by taking crypto from one user and providing it to another for a fee. The exact method of managing the loan changes from platform to platform. You can find crypto lending services on both centralized and decentralized platforms, but the core principles remain the same.

You don't just have to be a borrower, either. You can passively earn an income and gain interest by locking up your crypto in a pool that manages your funds. Depending on the reliability of the smart contract you use, there is usually little risk of losing your funds. This could be because the borrower put up collateral, or a CeFi (centralized finance) platform like Binance manages the loan.

How does crypto lending or crypto loan work?

Crypto lending typically involves three parties: the **lender**, the **borrower**, and a **DeFi** (Decentralized Finance) platform or **crypto exchange**. In most cases, the loan taker must put up some collateral before borrowing any crypto. You can also use flash loans without collateral (more on this below). On the other side of the loan, you may have a smart contract that mints stablecoins or a platform lending out funds from another user. Lenders add their crypto to a pool that then manages the whole process and forwards them a cut of the interest.

Types of cryptocurrency loan

Flash loans

Flash loans allow you to borrow funds without the need for collateral. Their name is due to the loan being given and repaid within a single block. If the loan amount cannot be returned plus interest, the transaction is canceled before it can be validated in a block. This essentially means that the loan never happened, as it was never confirmed and added to the chain. A smart contract controls the whole process, so no human interaction is needed.

To use a flash loan, you need to act fast. This requirement is where smart contracts come into play again. With smart contract logic, you can create a top-level transaction containing sub-transactions. If any sub-transactions fail, the top-level transaction will not go through.

Let's look at an example. Imagine a token trading for $1.00 (USD) in liquidity pool A and $1.10 in liquidity pool B. However, you have no funds to purchase tokens from the first pool to sell in the second. So, you could try to use a flash loan to complete this arbitrage opportunity within one block. For example, imagine that our primary transaction will take out a 1,000 BUSD flash loan from a DeFi platform and repay it. We can then break this down into smaller sub-transactions:

1. The borrowed funds are transferred to your wallet.
2. You purchase $1,000 of crypto from liquidity pool A (1,000 tokens).
3. You sell the 1,000 tokens for $1.10, giving you $1,100.
4. You transfer the loan plus borrowing fee into the flash loan smart contract.

If any of these sub-transactions cannot execute, the lender will cancel the loan before it takes place. Using this method, you can make profits with flash loans without any risk to yourself or collateral. Classic opportunities for **flash loans** include collateral swaps and price arbitrage. However, you can only use your flash loan on the same chain, as moving funds to a different chain would break the one transaction rule.

Collateralized loans

A collateralized loan gives a borrower more time to use their funds in return for providing collateral. **MakerDAO** is one example, as users can provide a variety of crypto to back up their loans. With crypto being volatile, you will likely have a low **loan-to-value ratio** (LTV), such as 50%, for example. This figure means that your loan will only be half the value of your collateral. This difference provides moving room for collateral's value if it decreases. Once your collateral falls below the loan's value or some other given value, the funds are sold or transferred to the lender.

For example, a 50% LTV loan of $10,000 BUSD will require you to deposit $20,000 (USD) of ether (ETH) as collateral. If the value drops below $20,000, you will need to add more funds. If it falls below $12,000, you will be liquidated, and the lender will receive their funds back.

When you take out a loan, you'll mostly receive newly minted stablecoins (such as **DAI**) or crypto someone has lent. Lenders will deposit their assets in a smart contract that may also lock up their funds for a specific time. Once you have the funds, you're free to do with them as you wish. However, you will need to top up your collateral with its price change to ensure it's not liquidated.

If your LTV ratio becomes too high, you might also have to pay fines. A smart contract will manage the process, making it transparent and efficient. At the repayment of your loan plus any interest you owe, you'll regain your collateral.

Advantages and disadvantages of crypto loans

Crypto loans have been commonly used tools in the DeFi space for years. But despite their popularity, there are some disadvantages. Make sure to take a balanced look before you decide to experiment with lending or borrowing:

Advantages

1. Easily accessible capital. Crypto loans are given to anyone who can provide collateral or return the funds in a flash loan. This quality makes them easier to acquire than a loan from a traditional financial institution, and there's no credit check needed.

2. Smart contracts manage loans. A smart contract automates the whole process, making lending and borrowing more efficient and scalable.

3. Simple to earn passive income with little work. HODLers can drop their crypto in a vault and begin earning APY without having to manage the loan themselves.

Disadvantages

1. High risk of liquidation depending on your collateral. Even with highly over-collateralized loans, crypto prices can drop suddenly and lead to liquidation.

2. Smart contracts can be vulnerable to attack. Badly written code and back-door exploits can lead to the loss of your loaned funds or collateral.

3. Borrowing and lending can increase the risk of your portfolio. While diversifying your portfolio is a good idea, doing so through loans will add extra risks.

Things to consider before getting a crypto loan

By using a trusted lending platform and stable assets as collateral, you'll have the best chance of crypto loan success. But before you rush into lending or borrowing, consider the following tips too:

1. Understand the risks of handing over custody of your crypto coins. As soon as the coins leave your wallet, you'll have to trust someone else (or a smart contract) to handle them. Projects can be the targets of hacks and scams, and, in some cases, your coins may not be immediately accessible to withdraw.

2. Think about market conditions before lending your crypto. Your coins may be locked up for a certain period, making it impossible to react to crypto market downturns. Lending or borrowing with a new platform can also be risky, and you may be better off waiting until it builds up more trust.

3. Read the loan terms and conditions. There's a vast amount of choice available of where to take out loans. You should look for better interest rates and favorable terms and conditions.

Famous crypto lending projects

Aave

Aave is an Ethereum-based DeFi protocol that offers various crypto loans. You can both lend and borrow, as well as enter liquidity pools and access other DeFi services. Aave is perhaps most famous for its work in popularizing flash loans. To lend funds, you deposit your tokens into Aave and receive aTokens. These act as your receipt, and the interest you earn depends on the crypto you are lending.

Abracadabra

Abracadabra is a multi-chain, DeFi project that allows users to stake their interest-bearing tokens as collateral. Users gain interest-bearing tokens when they deposit their funds in a lending pool or yield optimizer. Holding the token gives you access to your original deposit plus the interest earned.

You can further unlock the value of your interest-bearing tokens by using them as collateral for **a Magic Internet Money (MIM)** stablecoin loan. One strategy would be to deposit stablecoins in a yield-farming smart contract and then use the interest-bearing tokens to generate MIM. As long as your stablecoins don't experience volatility, the chances of liquidation will remain low.

Binance

Apart from its exchange services, Binance offers a range of other crypto financial products for users to lend, borrow, and earn passive income. If you don't want to access DApps and manage a DeFi wallet yourself, using a CeFi (centralized finance) option can be much easier. Binance gives access to simple crypto-collateral loans across many tokens and coins, including Bitcoin (BTC), ETH, and BNB. Funds for these loans come from Binance.

3. Yield Farming

Yield farming, or liquidity farming, is the act of lending or staking your cryptocurrency into a **liquidity pool**, through DeFi (Decentralized Finance) to receive rewards such as interest and more of their staked cryptocurrency. Similar to traditional staking, it can be seen as the equivalent of lending fiat money to a bank.

Interest rates or rewards rates are often measured in APY, which is the annual return rate of an asset, inclusive of compounding. The more frequently the interest compounds, the greater difference between the APY and APR of an investment. Banks and other more traditional investments usually stick to a flat APR.

Yield farming is often seen as the equivalent of Silicon Valley startups like Uber, which offer great incentives for early investors into the platform. New blockchain apps need liquidity to help sustain and eventually grow the platform, which is where yield farming steps in.

All staked cryptocurrency via yield farming is combined into a liquidity pool, usually for a specific pair of cryptocurrencies, such as CRO/ETH. These liquidity pools may be operated by Automatic Market Makers offering automated and permissionless trading tapping into liquidity pools instead of the generic buyers and sellers' system.

When investing in a liquidity pool, users will receive a Liquidity Pool token to keep track of their overall contributions to the pool. This LP token will represent the percentage of the liquidity pool the investor has provided and will be exchanged when you exit the pool.

Fact: The word 'farming' in yield farming comes from the farming analogy about 'growing' your cryptocurrency.

What is a Yield Farmer?

A crypto enthusiast with in-depth knowledge and a high tolerance for risk, continuously and relentlessly trying to optimize their yield by staking cryptocurrency. Yield farmers will often move to different pools every week, chasing the highest APY.

For example:

A yield farmer may make an initial investment into a farm using x token. They will receive some Y tokens for their participation.

They may then go and use their Y tokens on a liquidity pool that offers even more rewards, always trying to optimize their return.

How does Yield Farming work?

An investor will stake their cryptocurrency coins through a 'lending protocol' via a dApp (decentralized app on DeFi). Now that their liquidity is in, other investors can choose to borrow the liquidity for their own investments, trying to catch large swings in the staked coins' price.

As yield farming is used to reward early investors, often governance tokens of that blockchain will be given out to keep them as a user, and their liquidity in the system.

Governance tokens help keep a project decentralized and allow real users to vote on any new legislature. Governance tokens are at the core of any DAO or project which aims to be fully run by its users.

Liquidity pools essentially keep the ecosystem alive and are where most of the early liquidity will come from in smaller projects.

What are the Potential Rewards for Yield Farming?

Crypto yield farming first came available in 2020, and many yield farmers have bragged about triple-digit APY rates, unheard of outside of the crypto space. However, these rates bring volatility. Often, the tokens received as rewards from such farms are extremely volatile and prone to rug pulls. We will dive deeper into the risks of yield farming later in the article.

CoinMarketCap simply views this as a resource and investors are recommended to do their own research before dipping their toes into the volatile world of yield farming.

Many crypto yield farms with low impermanent loss risk continue to hold double-digit yearly APYs, with niche coin pairs and riskier farms reaching triple and even quadruple-digit APY returns, unsustainable but profitable in the short term.

Although almost all crypto trading is speculation, to consistently profit from yield farming, high-level strategies are usually required and a decent chunk of change is often recommended, even as a beginner.

Liquidity Mining

Usually, a crypto yield farmer will receive interest for their stake based on the APY. However, liquidity mining is when the farmer also receives a new token on top of their existing interest as a thank you for participation.

Risks of Crypto Yield Farming

Like anything in a purely speculative market like cryptocurrency, a higher tolerance for risk than normal is usually required, yield farming is no exception. Yield-farming is done only on Decentralized Exchanges (DEX) which leads to a multitude of potential risks.

Rug Pulls

Rug pulls occur when the developers or founders of a cryptocurrency decide to abandon a project, usually unannounced, by pulling the project's liquidity funded by investors. The investors keep their coins, but they are now worthless.

A rug pull is an **exit scam**, the founders have zero intention of returning to the project. Yield farmers are at a greater risk than normal to exit scams based on the type of startup cryptocurrency projects they are investing in, combined with the natural anonymity of crypto.

Smart Contract Bugs or Hacks

The most prominent risk in yield farming, smart contract risk occurs when bugs make the farmer's funds vulnerable to being hacked or stolen.

Impermanent loss

During the stake, the farmer's coins still follow the market value of that coin, meaning an investor can in theory lose a lot more than received through interest if their staked crypto drops a lot in value.

However, this can be argued that the farmer would not have sold even if they were not staking their coins, so at least they have gained some interest.

Volatility

On the same note as impermanent loss, dealing with extremely volatile cryptos can mean a skyrocket or plummet while your crypto is locked in a stake, and there's nothing you can do about it until the coins are released.

What are the Best Platforms for Yield Farming?

The general go-to platforms for yield farming are any well-known decentralized exchanges that support dApps. Good examples would be:

Uniswap
Pancake swap
Sushiswap
1inch Network

Please remember that DeFi has a much higher learning curve for new users than centralized exchanges, if mistakes are made, they can cost you dearly! Do your own research before jumping into any of these platforms!

1inch Network

The 1inch network is a great place for beginners to start their yield farming journey, as they pool the best rates and pools from all over the crypto sphere, meaning you will not have to manually hop around several different decentralized exchanges or dApps to find the best pools for you to provide liquidity.

1inch has a simple guide on how to start yield farming with them.
There is arguably no 'best' platform for yield farming. Each platform will allow yield farmers to operate on different chains, so doing your research before settling on one is your best bet.

Having a clear strategy before starting will allow the pieces to fall in place more smoothly and with less risk.

Is Yield Farming worth It?

To be truly successful at crypto yield farming, you not only must have a working strategy in place to maximize your yield and the initial capital to invest, but you must also be passionate about making passive income, actively.

Although you can simply stake in safe pools, the spirit of yield farming is to chase the best possible yields.

The key takeaway to deciding whether yield farming is worth it to you is, what do you want? Yield farming, especially on chains such as Ethereum with high gas fees is only viable for those looking to invest a considerable sum, otherwise, your initial investment will get eaten by gas fees.

4. Airdrop and Forks

A retroactive airdrop is the type of airdrop awarded to early users or people who have contributed to a project when an existing blockchain protocol is about to launch a native crypto token.

This type of airdrop is used to gather enough engagements on social media platforms by awarding tokens for retweets on Twitter, creating hype around the incoming token and also serving as a liquidity creation tool.

Takeover airdrops are used for a different reason entirely. Decentralized Finance (DeFi) protocols use takeover airdrops when they want to eliminate competition and attract more users or increase their user base by offering greater rewards than their competitors.

Takeover airdrops are always targeted at users who have engaged largely in activities such as staking. It also focuses on the liquidity providers to secure them from competing DeFi protocols. However, this is a more aggressive form of an airdrop compared to the retroactive form of airdrop.

What are Hard Forks and how do they work?

Blockchain protocols often suffer some changes that produce a new blockchain running in parallel with the original blockchain from which it is generated but the type of utilities it offers to the token holders and users may be different.

An example of a parallel blockchain is the **Bitcoin Cash** (BCH) fork, a P2P cash system created from what is called a **Bitcoin hard fork**.

Bitcoin forks are created by changing the base protocol code of a Bitcoin to create a parallel version of it, for an entirely different purpose.

A **hard fork** is the source of a new crypto token that creates value for the original investors through the native token of the newly created blockchain.

In August 2017, each Bitcoin holder received an equivalent amount of Bitcoin Cash (BCH) tokens which generated a good return, in relation to the $900 listing proof of BCH on many exchanges.

However, some hard forks were not created for a new system. Some originated from a crypto debacle.

An example is the Ethereum hard fork, Ethereum Classic (ETC) which has the native ETC token that can be exchanged freely on cryptocurrency exchanges and also supports different consensus mechanisms.

Hard forks can be of great benefit to investors than soft forks, with low risks through the increasing number of new blockchain protocols and new units being created.

Pros and Cons of Crypto Airdrop

There's no doubt that crypto airdrops are the catalysts for gaining traction to a new token. This method has been known to be used by developers to stimulate the adoption of their Crypto tokens.

Crypto firms who want to launch their native token for their DeFi protocol use airdrops to advertise their tokens due to their simplicity and cost-effective nature.

Though it involves expending a lot of tokens for free, it's only a small fraction of the tokens to be in circulation. It's surely an excitement to crypto token holders when they see users earn crypto from the free airdrops.

On the negative side, the market value and price of the token can drop if excess tokens are rewarded as airdrops.

Some addresses that got rewarded by the tokens can sell their tokens immediately after it is listed on the various crypto exchanges, this will cause a downward effect on the price of the token.

Pros and Cons of Hard Forks

Hard forks allow developers to feature new functionalities in the blockchain without changing the original blockchain which may have a user base that would counter the idea.

Token holders and investors who are issued extra hard fork tokens can monetize them immediately or hold them in anticipation of a long-run appreciation.

However, it may not always appreciate, just like the case of BCH which is trading near all-time lows since it was issued in 2017.

On the other hand, a hard fork occurs due to the splitting of the underlying blockchain. This is seen as detriment to the security of the network which renders the blockchain network more vulnerable to attacks. In this case, users of the hard fork token may face a bigger risk of losing their tokens in the light of any attack.

V. Participating in ICO token sales

The blockchain ecosystem offers a growing number of investors new avenues to make money. While many buy tokens or trade digital currencies, a new investment option involving **Initial Coin Offerings (ICO)** is now becoming common. With the popularity of ICOs undisputed, understanding how to participate in crypto ICO or knowing where to purchase ICO in a legitimate way often remains a challenge for many.

ICOs have the same fundamentals as **Initial Public Offerings (IPOs)**, however, with lower regulatory backing and varying dynamics to create your own cryptocurrency. Let's explore how to participate in an ICO as it is one of the lucrative ways of earning cryptocurrency.

Why invest in ICO tokens?

Every investor participates in token sales or owns cryptocurrency for various reasons. Using myself as an example, I hold some coins because I believe in the disruptive technologies they brandish. Unique projects with a visible use case conducting token sales may catch my attention, as many notably have, away from regulators. This was the case with the Ethereum Blockchain. To use the Ethereum platform for creating a smart contract, ETH is needed, and therefore, I purchased a few to put on my Ethereum wallet immediately.

However, everyone's goals differ, and only through a broad survey can we get to know the minds of investors. For what is most likely, Initial Coin Offering (ICO) tokens can present a whole new financial opportunity to investors per rate of gain. But before you turn into an investor yourself, you should understand, what is an ICO. In reality, ICO tokens are often sold at a relatively lower price compared to the price the tokens eventually list. This gives the investors a good return on their investments.

Depending on the problem the blockchain startup is aiming to solve, investors also exchange ICO tokens in order to gain access to the protocol and its products or services. For every varied reason each investor may have for backing a particular ICO, there is a feeling of being a part of an ecosystem designed to proffer solutions to a particular challenge. This sense of belonging is a vital reason why many invest in ICOs and also a good one to hold for those looking for a reason to join the train.

How to participate in ICOs?

Getting information about a prospective about an ICO is the first thing to do in order to be a part of the project. However, knowing about the token sale is not enough knowledge to secure an allocation. There are key things you must note before you can successfully participate in an ICO.

The process to participate in the ICO is described step by step below:

1. Decide where to buy ICO tokens (a trustworthy ICO exchange)

If there is one thing that is common in the digital currency world, it is the duplication of businesses with the same model. For instance, we have hundreds of new cryptocurrency exchanges, as much as there are thousands of coins and tokens. The space has a limited regulation and this draws in a lot of new projects to spring up. Therefore, always be aware of a potential scam.

This proliferation of platforms is why you must choose the ICO token exchange or platform carefully. Popular exchanges like Binance, Coinbase, Gate.io, Huobi, and Kraken amongst others typically offer a launchpad platform where new tokens raise capital through crowdsale. Amongst these options, you need to decide on which platform to pitch tents with.

On Coinmarketcap you can read all about new ICO coins on the market. If you have a particular presale, you have been following, the project may recommend a particular crowdfunding platform, in which case, you may not have the liberty to choose. The intent of choosing a crowdfunding platform is so that investors can do their due diligence in terms of registration.

Most token sale processes usually involve **Know Your Customer (KYC)**, and **Anti Money Laundering (AML)** checks. It is also good to decide where to buy your ICO tokens in advance as some platforms may not be available in your region due to regulatory compliance. Knowing which ICO exchange operates in your area will save you time in your ICO investment pursuit.

2. Set up your ICO wallet

After you must have registered on an exchange where you can purchase ICO tokens, you will need a funded account. As a crypto-related investment, you will need to have a wallet set up with the right cryptocurrency to participate in the token sale.

Most exchanges with launchpads offer an ICO wallet for their token sale process, however, those who do not often proffer a flexible option that prospective participants can explore. There is a likelihood that the majority of centralized exchanges with ICOs will offer a Bitcoin (BTC), Ethereum (ETH), or Stablecoin wallet to make your purchases in fiat currency, such as USD.

Once the wallet is up, you will need to fund the account either through a debit or credit card or via a P2P purchase system. Buying Bitcoin or Ether via credit card is a straightforward process that is similar to how general merchandise purchases are made online. The P2P system involves purchasing the coins you need directly from other sellers. More on P2P later.

It is not uncommon to open a third-party cryptocurrency wallet such as MyEtherWallet, Metamask, or Trust Wallet. These wallets are free from the prying eyes of exchanges and they support ERC-20 token formats as well as other new tokens which are typically used in ICOs today. The third-party wallets are better storage options for the ICO tokens when they are distributed. You can fund these wallets by transferring the right tokens for the sale from an exchange.

With your funded wallets with the right digital currency as specified by the token issuer, then you are good to go. Just keep in mind that storing also new coins and a hardware wallet always makes sense for safety reasons and not to share your private keys.

3. Learn how to buy ICO tokens at CoinList exchange

Token purchases and the underlying process may vary from one platform to another. It is important for intending token sale participants to understand the process of purchasing these tokens on their exchange of choice. So, let's learn how to buy initial coin offerings.

Let us take the popular token sale platform **CoinList** for example. The process involves pre-registration for the particular token sale program. Once you have agreed to the terms of the sale and verified that your country is not among the blacklisted nations, your registration will be approved.

On the token sale date, eligible participants are assigned a place in a waiting room for about an hour, and when the sale begins, each participant will be assigned a random number to enter the sale. When it is your turn, you will have a limited time to log in and make your purchase. The approved coins you can use for your purchases on CoinList include BTC, ETH, USDT, and USDC.

While the model of CoinList is fraught with sheer luck, it is one of the models out there. Other exchanges may require investors to join a Whitelist, and others may require you to stake their native token to gain access to the sales. It is the duty of the intending investor to do his own research about what is obtainable on his exchange of choice.

4.   Do basic diligence before you purchase ICO tokens

Token sales can be a very risky investment. It is advisable for prospective investors to do their due diligence before committing their capital. Unlike in the broader financial market where startups raise money through Initial Public Offering (IPO), there is no one to hold if the investment fails. This level of risk is why many governments go against plans to offer an ICO.

Based on this premise, investors can take their time to do the following before participating in an ICO;

Examine the whitepaper

Before committing your funds to any ICO, you must read, analyze and understand the project Whitepaper. These Whitepapers are crucial in communicating the visions of the project, the technology behind it, and the ways of implementing its laid-out goals. From the details in a Whitepaper, you can get a good glimpse of a project worth your time and money.

Analyze the team members

The team building a project based on blockchain technology should not be faceless. Know the team members, their qualifications, motivation, and general capability to execute the project. With the limited regulations in the crypto world, it is easy for any set of developers to group up, and launch a project with no sustainability model all to raise large amounts of money. Watch out for these and more fraudulent types of projects.

Analyze the project tokenomics

Token economics (tokenomics) is vital to predicting the potential success the project may brandish. Projects with bad tokenomics can end up marring the protocol, especially if the token is central to the functioning of the ecosystem.

5. Purchase the tokens

At this stage, you are certain you are participating in the ICO and you have the domiciled funds for this. Make the token purchase and complete any form of documentation that may be required. You need to be sure your payments are cleared and save any confirmation from the exchange account or platform confirming your payment/participation in the sale.

6. Join the protocol's social media communities

Most legit ICO projects often maintain a presence on social media which may range from Telegram, Twitter, Discord, and Facebook. It is ideal to join these communities for updates about the protocol development, new products, and ultimately, about the token you participated in.

Joining such forums helps you bond better with the team, as well as other investors. With this, you can be a true part of the ecosystem they are building, especially if you make use of the product and service on offer.

7. Claim/Receive your tokens

Different ICOs have different plans for the distribution of the purchased tokens. While some may be distributed after the sale to the ICO wallet you submit, others may have multi-month/year lockup periods. Either way, your participation in the ICO is not complete until you receive the tokens you paid for in your wallet.

Other tips on how to invest in ICO tokens safely & successfully

Altcoins

Check the track record of the launchpad

The success of every ICO is dependent on various factors, amongst which positive sentiment is one. This sentiment builds up with the track record of the prospective launchpad or ICO exchange that conducts the fundraising. An exchange with a good track record of successful ICOs post-launch is best than that which has no track record.

Avoid get rich quick schemes

There are ICOs that are best described as get-rich-quick schemes. These ICOs often make promises that are antagonistic to what their business model showcases. Investors should try as much as possible to avoid such ventures as capital may be at risk.

Reliance on influencer promotions should be low

As someone who has been a researcher and keen observer in the space, I can attest that it is very common for new projects to consult the services of social media influencers to promote their projects. These influencers need the money being paid to them and will decorate any project to the best of their ability. Reliance on YouTubers or other supposed influencers should be limited when planning to invest in a token sale.

Advantages and Disadvantages of Investing in ICOs

ICOs have a lot of benefits both for the companies and investors. However, they are also certain risks, which are worth considering before investing in ICOs. Let's walk you through some of the pros and cons of ICOs.

Advantages of ICOs

- It is a great way to invest early in a project.
- ICOs allow you to make huge profits in the long term.
- You can buy cryptocurrencies at discounted prices if you invest in ICOs.
- It is a fast and efficient method to raise funds for a startup crypto project.
- There are no restrictions to participating in an ICO. Anyone can participate in ICOs effortlessly.
- Crypto startups can raise a lot of funds in the early stage.
- The new project can reach a global audience with the help of ICOs.
- You can directly invest in the new projects without any middlemen.
- Participants can enjoy the benefits of being early adopters.

Disadvantages of ICOs

- Most of the crypto startups have low success rates, and the cryptocurrencies are volatile. Hence, there is a significant risk that a project will lose its value.
- If the project becomes unsuccessful, the funds you invested in the ICO will be worthless.
- Searching for a reliable project that has a huge potential is highly difficult, as numerous projects are being developed every day.
- ICOs are not regulated. There is a high possibility for an ICO to be a scam.
- Without a clear understanding of the crypto space and knowing how ICOs work, it is not advisable for new users to invest in ICOs.

Key takeaways on how to invest in ICOs

ICOs can be a very lucrative alternative to investing your capital in innovative blockchain projects. There are ways to get the most of the investments, and users must understand the demands from both the token issuers and the exchange platforms before committing their funds.

With numerous information flying around, investors should be active enough to do their own research before backing any project, either for the short or the long run.

VI. Exchange Traded Fund (ETF)

If you want to invest or speculate on the price of cryptocurrencies without actually buying any digital coins, buying units in cryptocurrency ETFs offer a way to do this.

ETFs allow you to track the price of an underlying asset or index, such as the price of a single cryptocurrency or a "basket" of several tokens – a convenient way of **diversifying your portfolio**. They also remove some of the barriers to entry, such as using a cryptocurrency exchange or learning how to store crypto safely. Another appeal is that ETFs are tightly regulated and offered through traditional platforms such as stock exchanges, including NASDAQ and the Toronto Stock Exchange.

Throughout cryptocurrency's history, ETFs have had a difficult time, with little support from regulatory bodies around the world. The **US Securities and Exchange Commission (SEC)** and other government regulators have typically rejected applications for Bitcoin-based ETFs. Because of this, there hasn't been a breadth of options for investing in such an index.

However, after years of lobbying, the SEC finally greenlighted official Bitcoin exchange-traded funds in October 2021. This was a significant development due to the globally available nature of US markets, which are typically accessible to investors in most parts of the world, while other local markets are not. The approval by the SEC has triggered a wave of applications for new cryptocurrency ETFs which are likely to expand beyond Bitcoin into other cryptocurrencies.

What is a cryptocurrency ETF?

An ETF is a collection (often called a "**basket**") of assets that can be bought and sold on a stock market the same way investors can trade ordinary shares in a company. ETFs are investment funds designed to track the performance of a particular index, such as the NASDAQ 100's QQQ, or a specific commodity or asset.

For example, a gold ETF allows you to invest in the value of gold without ever having to own any gold or find somewhere to store it.

Cryptocurrency ETFs are designed to give investors exposure to the cryptocurrency market. These indexes track the price of 1 or more digital coins or tokens. This lets investors add the value of crypto to their portfolio without some of the risks associated with actually owning any digital currency. Some of these risks include:

- **Custody**. While the vast majority of cryptocurrency exchanges hold funds on your behalf, some users are still nervous about the storage of cryptocurrencies. This may be due to the long history of exchange hacks, or a misunderstanding that they need to manage the coins themselves.
- **Regulation**. Most cryptocurrency exchanges are unregulated, although an increasing number are choosing to obtain relevant licensing. Despite this, user funds in most countries are not protected by the same protections as money in a bank account or stock trading platform.
- **Mistakes**. Cryptocurrencies are unforgiving – send funds to the wrong address and they are likely lost forever. While investors don't need to move cryptocurrencies from one address to another, the reputation for difficulty is still off-putting.

Cryptocurrency ETFs largely avoid most of these risks by taking custody of funds on behalf of investors and packaging them into a highly-regulated investment, which is served through traditional outlets, such as stock brokers.

The simplest way for a crypto ETF to track the price of a digital currency is for the ETF company to purchase and store that crypto, and then divide shares in the ownership of those coins between stakeholders. However, another model is for the fund to own futures contracts. These contracts allow investors to essentially "bet" on whether they think the price of a given cryptocurrency will rise or fall in a set period of time. **Futures-based cryptocurrency ETFs** were the first type to be approved by the SEC.

How do cryptocurrency ETFs work?

Broadly speaking, there are 3 types of cryptocurrency ETFs:

Physical-backed crypto ETFs

These hold actual coins and tokens which underpin the value of the ETF. If the value of the digital coins owned by the ETF rises, the value of your investment unit also increases.

- **Pros**. The most direct way of investing in crypto via an ETF, as the fund essentially just holds coins on your behalf. A good proxy for people who cannot or do not want to own actual coins.
- **Cons**. Still not as good as the real thing, with the ETF prices frequently lagging behind the market and trading restricted to market hours (unlike actual crypto which trades 24/7). Availability is also limited depending on what markets you have access to. For instance, in Canada retail customers can purchase physical ETFs, but in the US, they are regulated to accredited investors.

Futures-backed crypto ETFs

With this type of ETF, shares in the fund aren't based on actual coins but on futures contracts. A futures contract is an agreement that sets a fixed price and date for buying or selling an asset. As a result, they potentially allow investors to profit in both bearish or bullish markets (depending on the specifics of the fund). Futures-backed ETFs are typically used when holding the underlying asset would be problematic, such as storing barrels of oil, or safely securing cryptocurrency.

- **Pros**. This type of ETF is the first to receive approval for retail customers in the US. The fund is not directly exposed to the risks associated with storing cryptocurrency.
- **Cons**. Expensive compared to a physical ETF or real crypto. On top of the ETF management fees is the risk of contango, where futures contracts cost more than the underlying asset. This can cause futures-based ETFs to trade at a premium compared to the spot market, making them worse value for money than purchasing actual coins.

This type of ETF is quite different to the others as it is based on stocks of cryptocurrency or blockchain-related companies. The idea is to give exposure to the wider blockchain industry (the technology behind most cryptocurrencies) through a basket of stocks. For instance, the Bitwise Crypto Industry Innovators ETF is made up of **publicly traded exchanges** (Coinbase, Robinhood), **hedge funds** (Galaxy Digital), **mining firms** (Hut 8) and companies that **hold crypto in their treasury** (MicroStrategy, Tesla).

- **Pros**. A convenient way of gaining exposure to the wider industry through a mixture of companies. Likely less volatile than ETFs that track cryptocurrency prices and less overall risk.
- **Cons**. Less volatility also means less room for growth, compared to cryptocurrency-based ETFs. The cryptocurrency industry is still in the midst of regulation around the globe, which could negatively impact the prospects of some of the companies listed in these ETFs.

ETF units can be bought and sold on securities exchange markets, but brokerage fees apply. Just like shares traded on an exchange, the price of an ETF fluctuates throughout the day as investors buy and sell units. Keep in mind that ETFs only trade during market hours, while cryptocurrency trades 24/7. This can lead to a discrepancy between the price of the fund and the spot market.

You'll also need to pay a management fee to the ETF issuer, but this is included in the unit price. ETFs generally have lower fees compared to traditional managed funds (like a hedge fund), but higher than the cryptocurrency spot market.

Case study: How crypto ETFs work

To help you understand ETFs a little better, let's take a look at a hypothetical example.

The XYZ ETF is designed to track the performance of the world's five biggest cryptocurrencies by market cap – Bitcoin, Ethereum, XRP, Cardano and Binance Coin.

The company that issues the ETF owns a specified amount of each of the 5 currencies, and the ownership of these tokens is divided into shares. Investors then buy and sell those ETF shares on stock exchanges in the hope of benefiting from price increases to the underlying digital currencies.

Let's assume that the value of 1 unit of XYZ ETF is $50, and you decide to purchase 10 units for a total of $500. After 12 months of growth for global crypto markets, the XYZ ETF unit price has risen to $100, meaning your total investment is now valued at $1,000.

Had you taken a more traditional approach and decided to buy each of the 5 cryptocurrencies individually, you would have needed to create 1 or more wallets, registered for an account on a crypto exchange, paid brokerage fees for each individual crypto trade, and then tracked the price movements of each coin across the past year.

But with a cryptocurrency ETF, it's easier and far less time-consuming to gain access to a diverse portfolio of crypto assets

Benefits vs risks of Bitcoin ETFs

Just like any other type of investment, cryptocurrency ETFs have a range of pros and cons. It's essential that you weigh up the potential benefits against the risks involved before deciding whether you should invest in any crypto ETF.

Benefits

Simplicity. Learning how to buy and store cryptocurrency can be a difficult or nerve-racking process for some. ETFs make it simple to gain exposure to digital currencies without going through the hassle of owning any coins.

Accessibility. An increasing number of cryptocurrency ETFs are available through traditional stock brokers and exchanges. In addition to making them easy to access, they also come with the legal and regulatory protections associated with such services.

Diversification. Some ETFs offer a basket of various cryptocurrencies which streamlines the process of building a diverse portfolio. It prevents the need to purchase several currencies, which could involve multiple exchange accounts, wallets and technical understanding.

Security. Cryptocurrency exchanges and wallets are susceptible to hacking attacks and theft. Buying units in a crypto ETF protects you against these risks as you don't actually own any digital coins.

Risks

Limited choice. There's currently limited choice available for anyone wanting to invest in cryptocurrency-related ETFs, although this is rapidly changing. The world's most accessible ETF market, the United States, finally approved cryptocurrency-based ETFs in late 2021. It is likely that more ETF options will follow, but in globally accessible US markets as well as more local options.

Volatility. Cryptocurrencies are famous for their volatility and can experience substantial price fluctuations in a short space of time. If the market moves against you, the value of your crypto ETF units could take a sharp dive.

Lack of risk diversification. Traditional ETFs often include an extensive range of securities to help achieve diversification. They sometimes include government bonds and debt to mitigate market risk. However, most versions of crypto ETFs only provide access to a limited range of digital currencies. When you also consider the correlation between the performance of Bitcoin and the value of altcoins, this only increases the level of risk.

Crypto-specific risks still apply. Just because you don't have to deal with any of the risks of owning digital currency, that doesn't mean these risks cease to exist. Issues such as hacking will still need to be managed by the ETF provider.

Fees apply. On top of an annual management fee, you'll need to consider brokerage fees that apply when you buy or sell ETF units.

International taxes. If you buy ETF units located in another country be aware that foreign tax may apply.

Should you invest in an ETF or real crypto?

Cryptocurrency ETFs are best suited to people who want exposure to cryptocurrency markets, but do not want to or cannot own real cryptocurrency for various reasons.

This is because purchasing cryptocurrency directly, through a specialised cryptocurrency exchange or broker, is more cost-effective than investing via an ETF.

In addition to brokerage fees, which are typically higher than cryptocurrency exchanges, ETFs charge a management fee on top which is included in the unit price of the ETF.

They can only be traded during market hours – unlike crypto exchanges which operate 24/7. This means that the ETF will always lag behind the market, and prevent traders from capitalising on price swings outside market hours.

As such, ETFs are more suited to people looking for a long-term buy and hold investment rather than something to actively trade.

By purchasing an ETF instead of actual crypto, you are also missing out on the things that make it valuable – such as the option for self-custody, using it for payments, and earning interest.

That being said, if you want to invest in cryptocurrency markets without the responsibility of owning the actual coins or dealing with multiple exchanges or wallets, **then ETFs are one option.**

If you simply want to invest in coins in the hope the price rises, then a physically-backed ETF is likely what you want.

Alternatively, if you are a more experienced investor with a deeper understanding of markets, including futures, then you may want to explore a futures-backed ETF.

Lastly, if you are not interested in any specific coins, but are bullish on the sector in general, then a stocks-backed ETF could be a great way to diversify your investments across the whole market. Stocks-backed ETFs are also a way for the most die-hard of cryptocurrency investors to diversify their portfolio and gain exposure to sectors such as mining.

How to invest in a cryptocurrency ETF?

You essentially have 3 main avenues for investing in a crypto ETF, each with their own pros and cons. Keep in mind various ETFs are spread out over a number of providers, from brokers to privately managed funds. As such you will need to consider which markets you have access to when deciding on an ETF, in addition to the assets you actually want exposure to.

Purchase an ETF through a stock broker or exchange

1. **Use the table to choose an ETF that is traded via broker.** This means it is available to retail investors through a stock broker or similar service. Private funds are sold through the issuing company on an individual basis and typically restricted to accredited investors.
2. **Sign up for a broker that has access to the ETF you want.** For instance, if you plan on purchasing an ETF listed on NASDAQ or

the New York Stock Exchange (NYSE), you will need access to US markets, whereas ETFs listed on the Toronto Stock Exchange (TSX) require access to Canadian markets.

3. **Deposit funds and purchase the ETF**. Most platforms will allow you to purchase as little as 1 share, but keep an eye on the brokerage fees, which are charged either as a percentage or flat rate.

Purchase an ETF through a cryptocurrency exchange

1. **Use the table to choose an ETF that is available via a cryptocurrency exchange.** This means you can purchase and trade it on the exchange, just like you would with cryptocurrencies. Keep in mind that some exchanges offer ETFs, but only via private sale (see below).
2. **Sign up for the exchange by clicking on the name in the table.** You will likely need some photo ID and a webcam or smartphone to complete sign up.
3. **Deposit funds and purchase the ETF**. Deposit funds onto the exchange using your local currency or cryptocurrency. If the exchange only accepts cryptocurrency, then you will need to purchase a widely supported crypto like Bitcoin to trade for the ETF.

Purchase an ETF via private sale

Some ETFs are only available via private sale from the issuer, and come with certain requirements that leave them out of reach for the average investor. They are typically only available to accredited investors (or your local equivalent) and have a high minimum investment amount, often upwards of $50,000.

To purchase an ETF this way, you will need to go to the providers website and register your interest. Keep in mind that some funds have limited spots, so even if you meet the requirements you may not be able to purchase the ETF right away.

VII. Crypto-based Stocks

What are Crypto Stocks?

Crypto stocks are publicly traded companies that operate businesses that are highly exposed to the cryptocurrency market or blockchain technology.

These stocks include popular crypto exchanges, cryptocurrency miners, blockchain technology specialists and companies that have large cryptocurrency holdings on their balance sheets. They are typically highly correlated to cryptocurrency price fluctuations, making them extremely volatile and unpredictable.

Cryptocurrency investors and analysts generally expect the share prices of most crypto stocks to rise over the long term if cryptocurrency adoption and use continues to expand globally. But this type of volatile investment may not be suitable for all investors.

How to choose cryptocurrency stocks?

Cryptocurrency investors can balance high exposure to crypto markets and responsible risk management by identifying crypto stocks that have diversified, profitable business models and attractive valuations based on fundamental metrics such as price-to-earnings (P/E) ratio and price-to-sales ratio.

Investors can also identify crypto stocks that have leading market shares, positive analyst coverage and relatively low debt levels.

Where to buy cryptocurrency stocks?

The cryptocurrency stocks mentioned above all trade in the U.S. on the Nasdaq Composite or NYSE, making them easily accessible to anyone with an online brokerage account.

1. Mutual Funds

If you're looking for a convenient way to invest in crypto, a cryptocurrency mutual fund could be the solution.

Dear readers, as investors have flocked to digital assets, we've seen more and more **ways to invest in cryptocurrency**. One of the latest options is a **cryptocurrency mutual fund**. In this guide, we'll go over how cryptocurrency mutual funds work and where you can invest in them.

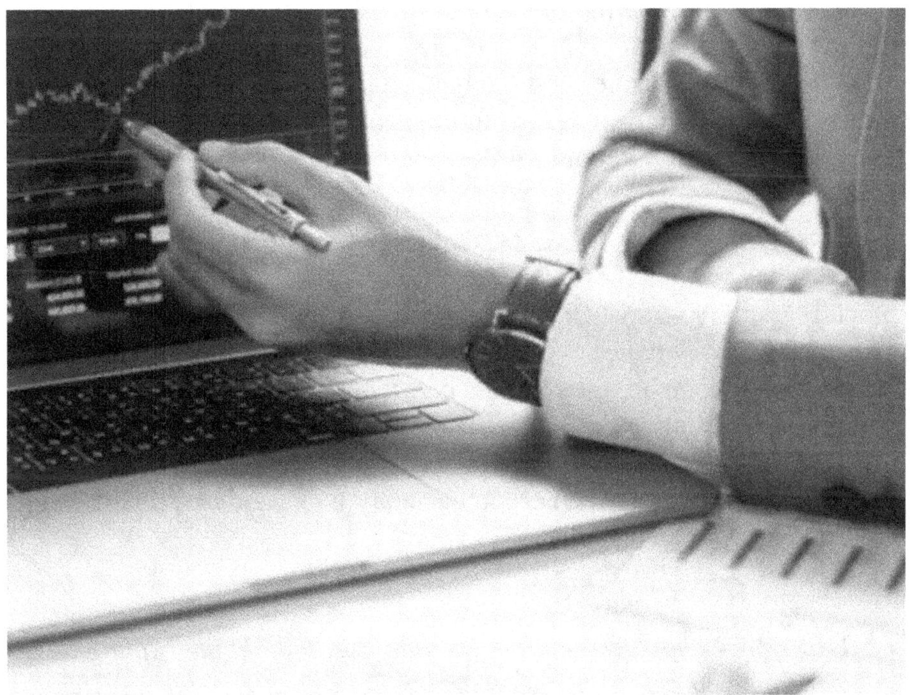

Image source: Getty Images.

What is a cryptocurrency mutual fund?

A cryptocurrency mutual fund is a collection of cryptocurrency assets packaged together as one investment.

If you're unfamiliar with mutual funds, they're professionally managed portfolios that include **stocks, bonds**, and **other securities**. Investors pool their money to invest in mutual funds. Because these funds contain a variety of assets, investors get a diverse portfolio in a single investment.

Each mutual fund has an **expense ratio**, which is the fee to invest in it. The expense ratio is a percentage of the assets under management.

Cryptocurrency mutual funds follow the same concept as traditional mutual funds. The difference is that they're designed to invest specifically in cryptocurrencies and assets tied to the cryptocurrency market. For example, a crypto mutual fund could invest in a balanced mix of several of the top types of cryptocurrencies. There aren't any that do that yet, though, due to Securities and Exchange Commission (SEC) regulations. Instead, funds invest in futures contracts tied to cryptocurrencies in an attempt to follow their price.

Cryptocurrency ETF vs. Cryptocurrency Mutual Fund

Cryptocurrency ETFs and cryptocurrency mutual funds are easy to confuse, because they have several similarities. A crypto ETF (exchange-traded fund) also pools investor funds, invests in a collection of assets, and charges an expense ratio.

The biggest difference between cryptocurrency ETFs and cryptocurrency mutual funds is how they're priced.

- ***ETFs*** *have share prices that fluctuate throughout the trading day. The time you place a trade affects the price you pay for an ETF.*

- ***Mutual funds*** *are priced once per trading day. All trades that process in a trading day have the same price, regardless of the exact time they were placed.*

Trading also works differently with ETFs and mutual funds. With ETFs, you buy and sell shares, just like with stocks. With mutual funds, you buy and sell specific dollar amounts.

Is there a cryptocurrency mutual fund?

There's currently one cryptocurrency mutual fund available to U.S. investors. **Bitcoin Strategy ProFund** (NASDAQMUTFUND:BTCF.X) was launched in July 2021 and is the first publicly available U.S. mutual fund designed to follow the results of **Bitcoin** (CRYPTO:BTC).

The Bitcoin Strategy ProFund invests in Bitcoin futures contracts. It requires a minimum investment of $1,000 and charges an expense ratio of 1.15%.

So far, U.S. investors don't have many crypto mutual fund options because mutual funds need to be registered with the SEC and are subject to its regulations. The regulatory agency has rejected many crypto funds over the years, citing the potential for fraud, volatility, and lack of investor protections in the crypto market.

The SEC has indicated it would be more receptive to futures-based crypto funds, and several Bitcoin ETFs were approved toward the end of 2021. Like Bitcoin Strategy ProFund, these ETFs attempt to track Bitcoin's results using futures contracts.

As far as funds that buy cryptocurrencies directly, no options have been approved in the U.S. yet. For now, the only options are futures-based funds.

Pros and cons to cryptocurrency mutual funds

Crypto mutual funds have their benefits and drawbacks. Here are the biggest advantages they offer:

- **They're easy to buy.** You can buy mutual funds with a brokerage account, so, like cryptocurrency stocks, they're a convenient way to invest in crypto. To buy most cryptocurrencies, you need an account on a crypto exchange.

- **They can help you build a diverse portfolio.** Mutual funds are a good way to diversify and reduce risk because they invest in a variety of assets. You can't really diversify much with crypto mutual funds yet due to the lack of options, but this should change if more funds are approved.

- **Cryptocurrency prices can go up very quickly.** The crypto market is known for large price movements. A crypto mutual fund could be one of your most profitable investments.

- **You can invest in them using tax-advantaged retirement accounts.** You can't buy Bitcoin directly with a retirement plan such as an IRA or a 401(k), but you could invest in a Bitcoin mutual fund.

Now, let's look at the most notable downsides with cryptocurrency mutual funds:

- **There are hardly any available.** Right now, there's only a Bitcoin mutual fund. If you're looking for a fund with a mix of different cryptocurrencies, you're out of luck.

- **Cryptocurrency is extremely volatile.** While you could make a lot of money from crypto, prices could also plummet. Investors normally buy mutual funds to reduce risk through diversification, but you're still taking on significant risk with a crypto mutual fund.

- **You don't own cryptocurrencies.** Since it invests in futures contracts, a crypto mutual fund's price may not entirely follow the price of its cryptocurrencies.

- **Expense ratios can be high.** The only example we have so far, the Bitcoin Strategy ProFund, charges 1.15%. Anything above 1% is considered on the high side.

How to invest in cryptocurrency mutual funds

If you're strictly looking for a cryptocurrency mutual fund, the closest option is Bitcoin Strategy ProFund. It doesn't invest directly in Bitcoin, but it invests in Bitcoin futures. You can buy it through a brokerage account.

Given the lack of options, you may also want to consider similar alternatives to crypto mutual funds. Here are a few of the closest types of investments.

Cryptocurrency trusts

An investment trust is a company that's set up as an investment fund. It offers a fixed number of shares, either privately or publicly, that investors can purchase. It pools that money and uses it to make investments.

Cryptocurrency trusts are investment trusts that focus on cryptocurrencies. They're similar to mutual funds in that they allow investors to take a more hands-off approach.

Grayscale is one of the largest companies offering cryptocurrency trusts. These include:

- **Grayscale Bitcoin Trust**(OTC:GBTC), which tracks the performance of Bitcoin.
- **Grayscale Ethereum Trust**(OTC:ETHE), which tracks the performance of Ethereum (CRYPTO:ETH).
- **Grayscale Digital Large Cap Fund**(OTC:GDLC), which tracks the performance of several of the largest cryptocurrencies by market cap.

Make sure to check out the fees before investing in a cryptocurrency trust. For example, the Grayscale trusts charge annual fees of 2% to 2.5%, so you're paying quite a bit for the convenience they offer. I will explain this in detail later.

Cryptocurrency ETFs

As I have already explained cryptocurrency ETFs are another type of managed fund that invest in cryptocurrency. They invest in crypto futures contracts and attempt to track the price of one or more digital assets. Here are a couple of the most well-known crypto ETFs:

- **ProShare Bitcoin Strategy ETF**(NYSEMKT:BITO) was the first cryptocurrency ETF approved by the SEC. It aims to track Bitcoin using Bitcoin futures contracts and has an expense ratio of 0.95%.

- **Valkyrie Bitcoin Strategy ETF**(NASDAQ:BTF) is a smaller Bitcoin ETF that also invests in Bitcoin futures contracts. It has an expense ratio of 0.95%.

Crypto-adjacent funds

If you're open to a more indirect method of crypto investing, you could look into what are called **crypto-adjacent funds**. These are mutual funds and ETFs invested in companies that work with cryptocurrency in some way. It's not the same as investing directly in crypto, but it gives you some exposure to that market.

Here are a few crypto-adjacent funds to consider:

- **Amplify Transformational Data Sharing ETF**(NYSEMKT:BLOK) invests in businesses that are involved in the blockchain technology that powers cryptocurrencies. It has an expense ratio of 0.71%.

- **Reality Shares Nasdaq NexGen Economy ETF**(NASDAQ:BLCN) aims to invest in companies that develop, research, or utilize blockchain technology. It has an expense ratio of 0.68%.

Cryptocurrency mutual funds are an intriguing possibility for the future, but they're still very much a work in progress. Between the crypto mutual fund and ETFs that are on the market right now, most only attempt to track Bitcoin, so you don't get a diverse mix of assets. If the SEC relaxes its stance on cryptocurrencies, it will likely lead to far more crypto funds and give investors more options to consider.

2. Index Fund

What is a crypto index fund, and how to invest in it?

A crypto index fund is a type of investment fund that holds a basket of cryptocurrencies, similar to a traditional stock index fund.
What is a crypto index fund?

In general, an index fund is a type of investment fund that aims to track the performance of a specific market index. In this context, a crypto index fund is a type of investment vehicle that aims to track the performance of a specific index of cryptocurrencies, such as the top 10 or 20 coins by market capitalization.

Crypto index funds are similar to traditional index funds, which track the performance of a specific stock market index, such as the *S&P 500*. The S&P 500 tracks the performance of 500 large, publicly traded companies in the United States.

Nonetheless, these funds are different from crypto exchange-traded funds (ETFs), which are similar to traditional ETFs in that they track a basket of assets (in this case, cryptocurrencies) and can be traded on a stock exchange. However, while traditional ETFs hold the underlying assets they track, crypto ETFs hold derivatives, such as futures contracts, that track the price of the underlying assets.

Examples of crypto index funds include **Grayscale's Digital Large Cap Fund**, which tracks the top 10 cryptocurrencies by market capitalization, and **Bitwise's 10 Crypto Index Fund**, which tracks the top 10 coins by market capitalization, weighting them by liquidity.

The main benefit of investing in a crypto index fund is that it provides investors with diversification. By investing in a basket of cryptocurrencies, rather than just one coin, investors are able to spread their risk across multiple assets. This can help to mitigate the volatility that is commonly associated with individual cryptocurrencies.

Another advantage of crypto index funds like Grayscale's Digital Large Cap Fund is that they are managed by professional fund managers, who are responsible for selecting the coins that make up the index and rebalancing the cryptocurrency portfolio as needed. This can help to reduce the time and effort required for individual investors to research and select individual coins to invest in.

However, since crypto index funds are still a relatively new and rapidly evolving asset class, and the regulatory environment surrounding them is still uncertain in many countries, it is important for investors to thoroughly research their chosen crypto index fund before investing.

How does a crypto index fund work?

A crypto index fund provides investors with a diversified portfolio of cryptocurrencies, which can help mitigate risk because if one cryptocurrency performs poorly, the other cryptocurrencies in the fund may perform well, helping to balance out the overall performance of the fund.

As mentioned, a crypto index fund is typically managed by a professional investment manager who selects a diverse portfolio of cryptocurrencies that aligns with the index or basket being tracked. The fund's performance is then closely tied to the performance of the underlying index or basket.

Investors can purchase shares in the fund, which gives them exposure to the underlying cryptocurrencies without having to purchase them directly. This can be ideal for investors who are unfamiliar with or uncomfortable purchasing individual cryptocurrencies.

Additionally, index funds are generally considered to be a more **passive investment strategy**, as the fund manager is typically not actively buying and selling the underlying assets.

The fund typically charges a management fee for professional management, and some funds may also have an expense ratio. The **management fee** is the fee charged by the fund manager to cover the costs of managing the fund, while the **expense ratio** is a percentage of the fund's assets that goes to cover other expenses, such as trading and custody fees.

Advantages and disadvantages of crypto index funds

Crypto index funds provide investors with a way to gain exposure to a basket of cryptocurrencies, rather than having to pick and choose individual coins to invest in. Some advantages of cryptocurrency index funds include:

- **Diversification**: By investing in a basket of cryptocurrencies, index funds can help spread risk across different coins and projects.

- **Professional management:** Index funds are typically managed by experienced professionals who make decisions about what coins to include in the fund and when to rebalance it.
- **Liquidity**: Since index funds are traded on exchanges, they can be bought and sold like any other asset.

- **Tax efficiency**: Index funds are tax-efficient and may even offer a tax advantage since only one index fund is kept rather than numerous individual equities, especially if they are kept in a taxable account.

However, there are also some disadvantages to consider:

- **Lack of control**: Investors in index funds have less control over their investments than those who own individual coins, as the fund's managers make the decisions about what coins to hold.

- **Higher fees:** Index funds often come with higher fees than buying individual coins, as there are costs associated with managing the fund.

- **Barrier to access**: Countries without cryptocurrency exchanges, which include many underdeveloped countries, do not permit access to crypto index funds. In addition, an underbanked or poor population cannot invest in index funds, even in nations with cryptocurrency exchanges.

- **Lack of knowledge**: Novice investors who lack the knowledge and expertise to pick individual coins may miss out on opportunities to invest in promising projects that are not included in the fund.

How to invest in crypto index funds

Investing in crypto index funds is a way to gain exposure to a diverse range of cryptocurrencies without having to manually select and manage individual assets. Here are the steps to invest in crypto index funds:

Research
Begin by researching the different crypto index funds available. Look for funds that have a good track record and are managed by reputable companies. Check the fund's historical performance and read reviews from other investors.

Choose a fund
Once you have identified a fund that you are interested in, you will need to open an account with the fund manager. This can typically be done online and may require you to provide some personal information and proof of identity.

Fund your account
After opening an account, a user will need to fund it with cash or cryptocurrency. The minimum investment amount may vary depending on the fund.

Buy shares
Once an account is funded, users can buy shares in the crypto index fund. The price of the shares will be determined by the fund's **net asset value**

(NAV), which is calculated based on the value of the underlying assets in the fund. An index fund's NAV moves almost exactly in tandem with the index it follows.

Monitor your investment

After buying shares in the fund, a user will need to monitor their investment and make sure that it is performing as expected. Some funds may allow users to trade shares on a secondary market, while others may require them to hold their shares for a certain period of time.

Track your gains and losses

Finally, users may want to track their gains and losses in the crypto index fund. This can be done by checking the NAV of the fund and comparing it to the price they paid for their shares.

Therefore, a few considerations before investing in crypto index funds like Grayscale's Digital Large Cap Fund involve the following:

- Knowledge about Grayscale's Digital Large Cap Fund and the cryptocurrency market in general: It is vital to understand the risks and potential returns associated with this type of investment.

- Review the fund's prospectus and other disclosure documents to understand the fund's investment strategy, fees and other crucial details.

- Open an account with a brokerage firm that allows you to invest in Grayscale's Digital Large Cap Fund. This can typically be done online.

- Fund your brokerage account with cash or securities. Be sure to check with your brokerage firm to understand its deposit requirements and any fees associated with funding your account.

- Place an order to purchase shares in Grayscale's Digital Large Cap Fund, which can typically be done online or over the phone.

- Monitor your investment and consider a plan for selling or holding your shares in the future.

Along with the above points, it is important to understand that Grayscale's Digital Large Cap Fund is an investment in a trust that holds a basket of digital assets, and it is not an ETF, so users must be aware of the differences before investing.

Crypto index funds vs. traditional index funds

Crypto index funds and traditional index funds are similar in that they both track a basket of assets and provide diversification for investors. However, there are some key differences between the two types of funds.

For instance, one major difference is the underlying assets that the funds track. Traditional index funds track stocks, bonds and other securities listed on traditional exchanges, while crypto index funds track cryptocurrencies listed on digital asset exchanges.

Another difference is the level of volatility and risk. Cryptocurrencies are known for their high volatility, meaning that their prices can fluctuate significantly in a short period of time. This makes crypto index funds riskier than traditional index funds.

Additionally, traditional index funds are regulated by government bodies, such as the Securities and Exchange Commission in the U.S., whereas crypto index funds are not yet fully regulated, which can pose additional risks for investors.

Are crypto mutual funds the same as crypto index funds?

Crypto mutual funds and crypto index funds are both types of investment funds that allow investors to gain exposure to the cryptocurrency market, but they have some key differences.

For instance, a crypto mutual fund is a type of investment fund that pools the money of multiple investors to purchase a diversified portfolio of cryptocurrencies. The fund is managed by a professional manager who makes decisions on what cryptocurrencies to buy and sell and when. The fund aims to provide a return on investment that is higher than the overall market.

On the other hand, a crypto index fund is a type of investment fund that tracks the performance of a specific index or benchmark of cryptocurrencies. The fund is passive and aims to replicate the performance of the index or benchmark it tracks, rather than attempting to outperform it. The fund is typically rebalanced periodically to ensure that it continues to match the performance of the specific benchmark.

Are crypto index funds good for investment?

Cryptocurrency index funds can be included in an investment portfolio by individuals who want to gain exposure to a broad range of digital assets, but don't have the time or expertise to select individual coins. Index funds are also considered a more passive investment strategy, as they are designed to track the performance of a particular market or index, rather than trying to beat it.

However, the cryptocurrency market is highly volatile, and there is a high risk of losing money. There are several risks associated with investing in crypto index funds, including lack of transparency and liquidity, risk of hacking, and limited regulatory oversight.

For instance, some crypto index funds may not disclose their holdings, making it difficult for investors to assess the risk of their investments, while others may be difficult to buy or sell, leading to illiquidity. In addition, cryptocurrency exchanges and wallets are vulnerable to theft and hacking, which can result in the loss of funds. Moreover, the cryptocurrency market is largely unregulated, which increases the risk of fraud and other financial crimes.

The future of crypto index funds

Crypto index funds are likely to see continued growth as more investors become interested in the cryptocurrency market and as the industry matures. Moreover, the increasing institutional interest in the crypto market is expected to drive the development of more sophisticated and diverse index funds and increased regulation in this area.

Additionally, the use of index funds could help to increase transparency and liquidity in the cryptocurrency market, making it more accessible to a wider range of investors. Overall, the future of crypto index funds depends upon the maturity of the cryptocurrency industry and, thereby, inclusion of such funds in an investment portfolio.

3. Cryptocurrency investment Trusts

As confidence has risen about bitcoin's ability to act as a secure long-term store of value, investors looking to preserve value and share it with future generations have become interested in including bitcoin in estate trusts. There are many benefits to including bitcoin in a trust, including reducing the risk of losing your bitcoin after death and ensuring your loved ones can benefit from its value and use. However, there are unique security concerns that must be addressed before investing bitcoin in a trust.

The Benefits of Investing Bitcoin in a Trust

There is value for both the managing investor and the beneficiaries of the trust to ensure that the wealth generated by long-term bitcoin investing is passed on to beneficiaries and loved ones. When done properly, investing bitcoin in a trust can reduce the risk of your bitcoin being lost after you die. It also keeps bitcoin out of probate, saving beneficiaries time and money, while keeping your bitcoin private and reducing the risk of exposure to digital attacks. Investing bitcoin in a trust means that the managing investor can ensure a trusted person can access and manage bitcoin, while creating clear instructions on how the bitcoin can be accessed and used, even after a death.

Beneficiaries Can Access Bitcoin Quickly

If bitcoin is distributed through a will, or if allocations are not made prior to death, the transfer of the bitcoin will be subject to a legal process known as **probate**. Probate is a legal process in which wills, property values, taxes, and debts are assessed and distributed to beneficiaries through a court of law. The probate process can take weeks or months, but the official value of the trust assets is assessed at the time of death.

Given the nature of Bitcoin price movement, the length of the probate process can have serious implications on the ability of beneficiaries to sell or otherwise gain access to the value of bitcoin. Holding bitcoin in a trust avoids the probate process, allowing beneficiaries to access the bitcoin much sooner. It also allows beneficiaries and the trust to avoid court costs associated with the probate process.

Bitcoin Holdings Remain Private and Secure

Another benefit of including bitcoin in a trust is the enhanced security it provides. The probate court process is public record, exposing your bitcoin holdings to anyone who is willing to read the court records. Trust documents are not public record; investing bitcoin in a trust prevents your bitcoin from becoming public record.

Another security concern for many investors is the potential for permanent loss of bitcoin after death. Bitcoin held in a non-custodial wallet does not have a paper trail or any other documentation that makes it easily recognizable in the event of sudden death. Hardware wallets are often inconspicuous, and there have been multiple instances of wallets being lost and never recovered simply because next-of-kin did not know that their existence, or they did not have the private keys necessary to claim ownership. Investing bitcoin in a trust relies on a trustee to be able to access and manage your bitcoin in accordance with your directive, reducing the risk of loss after death.

How to Invest Bitcoin in a Trust?

Overall, wisely investing bitcoin in a trust is no different than any other asset. It is imperative to always invest bitcoin in your trust according to your investment principles and goals. During your lifetime, establish best practices for long-term bitcoin storage in order to minimize the risks of digital or physical attacks. Finally, create a clear and thorough directive for disclosing and transferring control of bitcoin to beneficiaries that provides instructions on how less-experienced beneficiaries should manage their newly acquired bitcoin investment.

Prudent Investor Rule

Investing bitcoin in a trust requires careful consideration and observation of the prudent investor rule. Trust assets, including any gains and losses, typically impact the beneficiaries. The prudent investor rule requires the managing investor or fiduciary to manage assets as if they were their own, while considering the needs of the beneficiaries and avoiding unnecessary risk. Bitcoin is a volatile asset, and taking a high-risk position would violate the prudent investor rule and potentially cause harm to the beneficiaries

Prioritize Bitcoin Storage and Security

Investing bitcoin in a trust is inconsequential if the bitcoin is vulnerable to digital or physical attacks during your lifetime or during the transfer process. Ensuring proper storage and security of bitcoin, as well as methods for storing and accessing the associated private keys, is necessary to protect your investment and your beneficiary's ability to access the bitcoin. Long-term storage solutions, usually non-custodial or custodial cold storage, are the best method for storing bitcoin over the long term.

Create Clear Instructions for Transfer and Access of Bitcoin

As with other assets, it's necessary to have a clear and well-planned directive for transfer and use of bitcoin after death. Because knowledge of the private keys indicates the owner of the bitcoin, no court process or agency can declare your beneficiary the owner of your bitcoin if the private keys are lost. If you are utilizing an exchange or brokerage account to invest in bitcoin, ensure that your trust has a clear directive on transferring account ownership or control to your beneficiaries.

If your bitcoin is held in a non-custodial wallet, it's essential to have a clear directive that ensures the beneficiary will be able to access your private keys, which is the main method of identifying ownership of bitcoin. If your private keys are lost, your beneficiaries will not be able to claim or access any bitcoin in the trust. Because control of private keys means control of bitcoin, it's important to have a clear and secure method of protecting your private keys prior to transferring control, as well as during the transfer process, so only the beneficiaries of the bitcoin assets know the private keys.

*Now let's see the cryptocurrencies trust as a **means of investment***

Grayscale Bitcoin Trust (GBTC)

Grayscale® Bitcoin Trust (GBTC), an investment trust that's traded on the stock market, is a great option for individuals, companies and institutions unfamiliar with the crypto world who want to invest in Bitcoin without directly managing it.

But is it a good investment option for everyone else? Are you missing out if you haven't invested in it yet? Are there drawbacks that might deter some people from buying Grayscale?

What is Grayscale Bitcoin Trust?

Grayscale Bitcoin Trust (GBTC) is the world's largest Bitcoin fund. It's also the **first-ever publicly traded trust** that has a digital currency as its underlying value. If you don't know what that is, here's a quick rundown.

Trusts and funds on public stock exchanges have an underlying asset that dictates their value. These assets are mostly stocks in publicly traded companies. The price of the trust or fund fluctuates based on the underlying **net asset value (NAV)**, which is affected by the asset's demand. An investor can buy a portion of the asset by purchasing shares in the fund.

Since GBTC is a cryptocurrency trust, you can buy its shares through your brokerage account. In doing so, you indirectly buy Bitcoin — avoiding the hassle of purchasing BTC through a crypto exchange. This means that you're relying on Grayscale to buy and hold Bitcoin for you as a third party.

So, the actual BTC is stored in the Grayscale institutional trust, and its retail index is traded on either the open or over-the-counter market. GBTC is similar to a crypto exchange-traded fund (ETF), as it pools investors' funds to invest in Bitcoin and charges investors a management fee for investing in the fund.

How Does the GBTC Investment Vehicle Compare to a Bitcoin ETF?

Essentially, a Bitcoin ETF, such as the Purpose Bitcoin ETF, is a competitor of GBTC. That's because ETFs track the market data or value of the underlying asset much more closely than a trust. Hence, the market price per Bitcoin ETF share is relatively close to the actual value of BTC.

But that's not the case with shares of GTBC, because the trust charges a 2% management fee and sometimes also a premium. That significantly increases the price of a GBTC share as compared to the market price of BTC while spot buying, or while buying shares of a Bitcoin ETF.

However, there are currently only Bitcoin futures ETFs in the market. GBTC is proposing to be approved as a *Bitcoin spot ETF*, which may be a better product than *Bitcoin futures ETFs* — as spot Bitcoin ETFs track the market even more closely than Bitcoin futures ETFs.

How Grayscale Bitcoin Trust (GBTC) Works?

Grayscale Bitcoin Trust gathers money, usually U.S. dollars (USD), from institutional investors and uses that to buy BTC directly. These BTC are stored in the Grayscale fund, which essentially makes the Grayscale institution — rather than its investors — the actual owners of BTC. You can then buy shares of GBTC and indirectly own BTC.

Ever since Grayscale became a publicly traded fund in 2015, various investors have poured a lot of cash into GBTC by buying Grayscale stocks during bull market cycles. Grayscale has used that capital to buy more and more BTC. Now, it's accumulated over 626,110 bitcoins, which is around $18.8 billion in assets as of the time of this writing (Sep 2023).

To put that number into perspective, Tesla holds approximately 10,725 bitcoins and Ukraine holds about 46,000 BTC.

What are Premiums and Discounts on GBTC Shares?

When you buy or sell GBTC shares, the trust doesn't immediately buy or sell BTC with your investment. That's where the concepts of premium and discount come into play, which are essential to learn about if you want to understand how GBTC works.

Suppose the Grayscale trust has about 500,000 BTC, which are all bought by shareholders. Then five investors come in, and each buy 1,000 BTC worth of GBTC shares.

Those purchases will raise the overall value of the trust by increasing the number of BTC held by GBTC investors as compared to the number of bitcoins owned by Grayscale as an institution. That's because GBTC doesn't immediately use the new investment to buy 5,000 more BTC.

This means that there's a greater demand for GBTC shares than the supply of BTC. In such a case, the trust will add a premium to BTC's value. Anyone who wants to buy GBTC shares will then have to pay that premium on top of the share value.

Similarly, if a bunch of investors sell their GBTC shares, the new investors will get a discount. This fluctuation means that you have to buy BTC at a different price than what you'll get by buying directly from exchanges. That's why GBTC share prices aren't the same as the actual value of BTC.

Finally, you can only buy or sell GBTC shares during the opening hours of the stock market, unlike BTC spot buying and selling, which you can do at any time.

Pros and Cons of Grayscale Bitcoin Trust (GBTC)

To help you decide whether or not to invest in the Grayscale Bitcoin Trust, let's look at its pros and cons.

Pros

Some advantages of buying GBTC stocks over owning Bitcoin directly include:

1. More Security in Cold Storage

Crypto exchanges and wallets are vulnerable to hackers and scams. GTBC charges a management fee for keeping their BTC secure in cold storage, which is safe from hacks.

2. Regular Audits of the Bitcoin Investment Trust

The Grayscale Bitcoin Trust files audited reports with the securities and exchange commission (SEC) to prove that it has the BTC that investors have paid for. That's an advantage over crypto exchanges, which have the potential to scam people. An example of one such scam is the QuadrigaCX exchange scandal of 2019.

3. Tax Advantages

Investors can get tax breaks when they buy GBTC shares through tax-advantaged accounts, such as a 401(k) or an IRA. It's also easier for investors to file taxes for publicly traded stocks of a trust that's approved by the SEC.

Cons

Some drawbacks of owning GBTC stock are as follows:

1. Not Suitable for Smaller Investors

GBTC charges a 2% annual fee. On top of that, you have to pay a premium to buy shares when demand is high. It's not a good fit for smaller investors, because you need a minimum investment of $50,000 to buy into Grayscale Bitcoin Trust.

2. You Never Actually Own Any BTC

You can never redeem your shares for actual BTC because the Grayscale trust owns the private keys to the BTC in your shares.

3. The Ever-increasing Performance Gap

The value of a GBTC share hasn't been growing at the same rate as its underlying asset. Even if you don't have to pay a premium, you still won't earn as much profit by buying shares as you will by owning Bitcoin directly. From 2020 to 2021, when bullish market happening, GBTC's share price increased by approximately 220% in value while BTC surged by nearly 340%.

4. Refusal to Share Proof of Reserves

On November 19, 2022, Grayscale stated that it would not be sharing its proof of reserves (PoR) with its customers due to security concerns, despite the global panic over the FTX implosion. This refusal has sparked public furor over the company's future.

Is Grayscale Bitcoin Trust a Good Investment?

GBTC isn't a good investment option because the value of GBTC shares doesn't accurately match the value of Bitcoin. Its shares have been trading at a discount since early March 2021, and they're now trading at a record low 45.08% discount to Bitcoin's net asset value.

So, if you buy GBTC shares today, you'll get fewer BTC than what you'll get through spot buying for the same amount of USD.

Investing in GBTC doesn't give you voting rights on protocols, because you don't own the private keys to the BTC in your shares. Also, transactions occurring on the trust are censored by government agencies — which defeats the original purpose of a decentralized digital currency.

Perhaps in the future, if the shares start trading at a premium again, then Grayscale will be a good option for accredited investors who can purchase GBTC shares at the NAV price.

Buying GBTC vs. Buying Bitcoin

Volatility is unavoidable whether you're buying BTC directly or on the open market through GBTC. Whenever lawmakers release new rules about regulating crypto, or deny a crypto ETF request, GBTC's share prices take a bigger nose dive than Bitcoin's market price.

Also, since you don't own the BTC in your GBTC shares, you can't use it. If you want to actually use Bitcoin and save on management fees, then you're better off buying BTC directly.

VIII. Investing in a cryptocurrency Roth IRA

Roth IRAs are retirement investment accounts that offer tax-free investment growth and tax-free withdrawals.

Pro Tip:

Roth IRA retirement savings accounts offer lucrative tax benefits in the future.

For those eligible, a Roth IRA allows the money contributed to grow tax-free, with no tax on distributions.

IRAs have annual contribution limits of $6,500 in 2023 (plus an extra $1,000 for those 50 or older).

Roth IRA meaning

A Roth IRA is an Individual Retirement Account that has special tax advantages: Distributions from the Roth IRA in retirement are **tax-free,** because the money contributed is taxed. You can withdraw contributions to a Roth IRA without tax or penalty.

This is unlike a traditional IRA, which offers a tax deduction when you contribute but requires taxes owed on distributions in retirement.

How does a Roth IRA work?

You contribute to a Roth IRA with after-tax dollars, which essentially means there is no immediate tax deduction or other tax benefit for contributing to the account. Once your account is funded, you can invest that money through the Roth IRA. Over a long time, horizon, those investments will likely earn a return.

That's when the real benefit of the Roth IRA kicks in: Qualified withdrawals from the Roth IRA during retirement (defined here as after age 59 1/2) are tax-free, because you didn't receive a tax benefit when you funded the account. This includes all of the investment growth we just referenced, which would otherwise be taxed.

Additionally, because you paid taxes on the contributions before putting them into the Roth IRA, you can withdraw those contributions — but not investment earnings — at any time without additional taxes or penalties from the IRS.

Your Guide to Crypto Roth IRAs

Would you like to avoid hefty capital gains taxes while building wealth with cryptocurrency investments? Investing in a crypto Roth IRA might be one of the easiest ways to do this.

Roth IRAs are funded with after-tax dollars, so your investments can grow tax-free until you're ready to withdraw them after retirement (but not before you reach the age of 59½). After that, all withdrawals made from your Roth IRA are completely tax-free.
Since regular crypto investments are subject to capital gains taxes, self-directed IRAs can be a great way to diversify your retirement savings and build your cryptocurrency portfolio in a tax-advantaged way.

What are Crypto Roth IRAs?

The IRS has been taxing cryptocurrencies as property since 2014. This means, from a legal standpoint, they fall into the same category as stocks, bonds, and other investment assets.

You can't place any of these investment assets (including cryptocurrencies) directly into your Roth IRA. This is because Section 408(a)(1) of the Internal Revenue Code of 1986 states that all contributions to an IRA must be made in cash.

So, to invest in crypto through your Roth IRA, you'll need the help of a custodian. This is usually a financial institution tasked with keeping your IRA investments safe and complying with all government regulations. The problem is that despite the growing popularity of cryptocurrencies, few custodians are willing to accept crypto in an IRA. However, you can overcome this problem by opting for self-directed IRAs, which are designed to hold alternative assets like cryptocurrencies.

A crypto Roth IRA, therefore, is simply a self-directed IRA that includes cryptocurrencies in its portfolio of assets. There are two main types of crypto Roth IRAs that you can invest in.

- **Checkbook Roth IRA:** With this type of IRA, you'll have the freedom to invest in many different types of alternative assets, including cryptocurrencies. You can also diversify your investment portfolio with real estate, tax liens, gold and other precious metals, etc.
- **Dedicated Crypto Roth IRA:** This type of IRA is designed specifically for the purpose of investing in cryptocurrencies. So, if you open a dedicated crypto Roth IRA, you can't use it to invest in any assets other than cryptocurrency.

Can you Stake Crypto in a Roth IRA?

Crypto staking involves pledging a portion of your digital coins to the cryptocurrency protocol for a given period of time. In exchange for this contribution to the blockchain network, you can earn additional coins or crypto tokens as a reward.

For the sake of simplicity, you can think of 'staking' as the crypto equivalent of depositing money in a bank. Just as you'd earn interest for locking up your money in a certificate of deposit (CD), you can earn rewards for locking up a portion of your crypto assets to confirm transactions on the blockchain.

Cryptocurrencies like Solana and Cardano – which use the proof-of-stake (PoS) model to process payments – require staking the most.
You can earn up to 5-20% staking rewards by opening a self-directed IRA LLC.

As of now, the IRS has not issued any specific tax guidance on staking transactions conducted through a Roth IRA. Crypto mining – which is an activity similar to staking in many ways – may be taxable within a Roth IRA and subject to unrelated business income tax.

Crypto IRAs vs. Other IRA Types

Self-directed crypto Roth IRAs are just one among many different types of individual retirement accounts. Some of the other popular IRA options are:

Traditional IRA

This is one of the most popular types of IRA. Currently you can get an upfront tax break by contributing up to $6,000 in a Traditional IRA (or $7,000 if you're 50 or older). In addition, all contributions made to a Traditional IRA are deductible, which can help lower your taxable income for the year. This type of IRA is perfect if you believe that your tax bracket during retirement will be lower than it is now. It's also a good option if you don't have access to a workplace-sponsored retirement plan.

Spousal IRA

This is the best IRA option for married couples where one of the spouses has either no or very low income. Typically, a person must have earned income to be able to contribute to an IRA. However, if you're a stay-at-home parent married to someone who has a regular income, then you can use your spouse's earnings to fund a separate IRA for each of you. The contribution limits are the same as for a Traditional IRA.

SEP IRA

The Simplified Employee Pension (SEP) IRA might be the best option for small-business owners who'd like to avoid the massive costs associated with starting and operating a conventional retirement plan for employees. SEP IRAs are set up and funded by an employer for their employees. The contribution limit in 2023 is $66,000, and the employer receives a tax benefit for the amount contributed. The contribution for each employee account is calculated as a percentage of salary.

The Difference – An Overview

The primary difference between the types of IRA mentioned earlier and a self-directed crypto Roth IRA is the types of assets or investments that can go into the account.

The traditional SEP and spousal IRAs typically allow only common investment vehicles like stocks, bonds, exchange-traded funds (ETFs), and mutual funds.

A **self-directed crypto Roth IRA**, on the other hand, can be used to invest in a wide range of cryptocurrencies like Bitcoin, Ethereum, Solana, Cardano, and many more.

Unless the self-directed IRA is dedicated solely to cryptocurrencies, you can also use it to invest in other alternative assets like gold, real estate, and privately held companies.

Another difference is that self-directed crypto Roth IRAs allow account holders to control their own investment decisions. In traditional SEP and spousal IRAs, on the other hand, all investment decisions are made by the plan administrators tasked with overseeing the account.

As a result, the holders of crypto Roth IRAs can take the reins of their own retirement planning and make investments in Bitcoin, Komodo, Ethereum, and other renowned as well as obscure cryptos.

Can you use your Roth IRA to buy Cryptocurrency?

Yes, you can buy cryptocurrencies using your Roth IRA under the following conditions:

- You've opened a self-directed Roth IRA since most regular IRAs won't allow crypto investments.
- The self-directed IRA is crypto-compatible, meaning that it either holds cryptocurrencies exclusively or along with other alternative assets.
- You've transferred funds to your IRA in cash and then used those funds to buy crypto. You can't place crypto in a Roth IRA directly.

If you'd rather not deal with all the technicalities involved in the process of buying crypto through your Roth IRA, you can opt for a reputed full-service cryptocurrency IRA platform like **Bitcoin IRA**.

This platform will help make the process of investing in crypto through a Roth IRA much easier, safer, and more convenient. Bitcoin IRA was founded to help Americans achieve their retirement goals through cryptocurrency investments.

Some of the benefits that this platform offers investors are as follows:

- World-class security features, such as a multi-signature digital wallet and 100% offline cold storage of digital currencies.
- A helpful and competent support team providing full, 24/7 phone support.
- Custody insurance coverage of up to $700 million from BitGo Trust.
- Many useful features for crypto investors, such as live price tracking and portfolio performance reports.
- Bitcoin IRA allows you to buy and sell over 60 cryptocurrencies through your Roth IRA.

So, if you'd like some help growing your retirement funds with a crypto Roth IRA, then you can simply navigate to the Bitcoin IRA website and open an account (use https://bitcoinira.com if you are reading the hard copy of my book) in a few simple steps.

Advantages of Crypto Roth IRAs

Investing in a crypto Roth IRA can provide you with three major benefits. We'll discuss them in greater detail in this section.

Portfolio Diversification

Cryptocurrencies like Bitcoin and Ethereum are not tied to the stock market, so they can infuse your retirement portfolio with some much-needed diversification in the event of an economic downturn or stock market crash.

If your Roth IRA contains nothing but stocks and mutual funds – as is often the case with Traditional IRAs – then you might lose a significant portion of your retirement savings if the stock market were to falter. Adding some alternative assets like crypto, gold, and real estate to your Roth IRA will help you stay financially stable even during a market downturn.

Tax Savings

As mentioned before in this article, Roth IRAs are funded with after-tax dollars. So, if you buy cryptocurrencies through your crypto Roth IRA, you won't have to pay any capital gains tax on these trades.

This is because the funds in the Roth IRA had already been taxed before they were used to buy the cryptocurrencies. If cryptocurrencies experience significant growth in the future, this could result in huge tax savings for you when you're ready to retire.

Growth Potential

If cryptocurrencies become more accessible and continue to grow in popularity over the next few decades, then they can prove to be an excellent investment for the future.

While many consider crypto to be a risky investment at present, they (and the blockchain technology on which they're built) also present a chance for unprecedented growth and wealth creation.

This is why more and more investors are choosing to grow their retirement savings by purchasing digital coins through a self-directed crypto Roth IRA.

Disadvantages of Crypto Roth IRAs

The primary disadvantages of a self-directed crypto Roth IRA are the risk and price volatility associated with cryptocurrency.

For most people, their retirement savings will determine their comfort and security during their senior years. Hence, the safety of the funds held in a Roth IRA is of great importance.

Self-directed IRA providers, however, are not bound by the broker fiduciary duties that usually hold Traditional IRA providers accountable. So, it's up to you as the investor to properly assess the risks and rewards associated with the crypto market. If you make a mistake in your assessment, you stand to lose a huge portion of your retirement savings. Furthermore, most cryptocurrencies – including the biggest ones like Bitcoin – often experience extreme price fluctuations. This makes them an unsuitable investment type for retirement planning, especially if you're close to reaching retirement age.

Is a Crypto Roth IRA right for you?

To determine whether or not a self-directed crypto Roth IRA would be a good way to build your retirement savings, you need to consider a handful of factors.

- **Age:** Cryptocurrencies are a volatile asset that often experiences massive price fluctuations, so you should only invest in them if you're young and have many decades before retirement. This is to ensure that a sudden fall in the price of bitcoin won't plunge you into poverty after retirement.

- **Risk Appetite:** Since cryptocurrencies are not the most stable and mainstream investment vehicle, you need to have a relatively large risk appetite to consider using them for your retirement planning. A crypto Roth IRA might not be the right choice for risk-averse investors.

- **Knowledge:** You should have a deep understanding and knowledge of the crypto market before setting up a self-directed crypto Roth IRA, as self-directed IRA providers are not bound by the same broker fiduciary duties that bind Traditional IRAs.

Where to open a Crypto Roth IRA

If you want to open a self-directed crypto Roth IRA quickly, safely, and in a hassle-free manner, then you should consider opening an account with Bitcoin IRA. It's the first and most trusted crypto IRA platform that aims to help Americans build their retirement corpus with cryptocurrencies.

To this end, it offers more than 60 cryptocurrencies for investors to choose from, 24/7 crypto trading facilities, and an option for tracking the prices of various digital currencies in real-time. Bitcoin IRA was designed to make the process of opening and operating a crypto Roth IRA as easy as possible.

IX. Peer to Peer (P2P) trading

What is Peer-To-Peer Trading and how do people use it?

Peer-to-peer (P2P) trading is the direct buying and selling of cryptocurrencies among users without intermediaries. P2P exchanges connect buyers and sellers and provide a layer of protection through escrow services, feedback / rating systems, and dispute resolution.

The advantages of P2P trading include global accessibility, multiple payment options, zero transaction fees, and personalized offers. However, it also has drawbacks, such as slower trading speeds and lower liquidity than centralized exchanges (CEXs).

In this article, we will discuss the pros and cons of P2P trading and how people can benefit from it.

What is P2P Trading?

P2P crypto trading refers to the direct buying and selling of cryptocurrencies among users, without a third party or an intermediary. This is unlike buying and selling cryptocurrencies using a CEX, where you cannot transact directly with counterparties.

A CEX would use charts and market order aggregators to gauge the current market prices and determine the optimal time to buy, sell, or hold your crypto. When you are ready to buy or sell, the exchange enters your order into its order book and facilitates the transaction on your behalf.

Depending on the type of order you use, effects such as **slippage** may mean you don't get the exact price you want. P2P trading, on the other hand, gives you full control over pricing, settlement time, and whom you choose to sell to and buy from.

How does a P2P exchange work?

Think of a P2P exchange in the same way you might Facebook Marketplace — they are similar in that they both connect buyers and sellers. However, buying or selling something on Facebook Marketplace can be tricky as the counterparties are strangers and it's difficult to establish trust.

What happens if the seller receives payment, then proceeds to block the buyer and not mail them the product that they purchased? In this instance, the buyer loses money due to fraud.

P2P exchanges aim to not only connect buyers and sellers, but also provide them with a layer of protection by securing transactions and reducing the risk of fraud. Buyers and sellers can browse crypto ads and post their own ads while enjoying this protection, made possible by feedback and rating systems.

In addition, the P2P exchange uses **escrow** to secure the crypto being bought and sold until both parties have confirmed the transaction. For example, if you are selling bitcoins for fiat money, Binance will escrow your BTC. Once you receive the fiat money, you can confirm the transaction and the BTC will be released to the buyer's wallet.

If either party is dissatisfied with the transaction, they can_file an appeal to resolve the issue with the counterparty, or have_Binance Customer Support step in. Do note, however, that the appeal must be filed during the order process, while the order is still pending.

Advantages of P2P Trading

Global marketplace

One advantage of using a local P2P cryptocurrency exchange is that it gives you access to a global market of cryptocurrency buyers and sellers. For example, some P2P exchanges are accessible in hundreds of countries, allowing you to buy and sell cryptocurrencies with people around the world in a matter of minutes.

Multiple payment methods

Traditional exchanges may not offer as many payment options as P2P exchanges. Binance P2P, for example, offers over 700 payment methods, including in-person cash payments. This can be useful for those who prefer face-to-face transactions or those without access to a bank account.

Zero trading fees for takers

While some cryptocurrency exchanges charge a fixed fee or percentage per trade, others allow traders to connect and conduct transactions for free — be sure to check the terms and conditions before deciding on a P2P exchange.

Secure transactions via escrow

As mentioned above, some cryptocurrency exchanges use escrow services to protect both buyers and sellers. When choosing to secure a transaction with escrow, funds are held by the exchange and released only when the terms of the transaction are met by both parties.

Transactions must be completed within a certain time frame; if a buyer doesn't make the fiat payment within the specified time, their order is canceled and the cryptocurrency is returned to the seller's wallet.

Personalized offers

Sellers have complete control over the selling price, exchange rate, payment method, and how much they are willing to sell per transaction. The same is true for buyers (buying price, payment method, and how much they are willing to spend per transaction). As long as both parties' terms align, a deal can be struck.

Disadvantages of P2P Trading

Slower trading speeds

While a P2P transaction can be conducted almost instantly once both parties have confirmed the transaction, one party might delay the transaction for various reasons. With traditional trading, you don't have to wait for the buyer or seller to confirm the transaction before you can move on.

Low liquidity

P2P exchanges naturally have lower liquidity than CEXs due to the nature of the process. For this reason, larger traders who need to complete major transactions may prefer to use over-the-counter (OTC) trades, or buy / sell via the standard exchange.

How do people benefit from trading P2P?

P2P trading is a convenient way to invest in cryptocurrency. Not only does it allow you to buy or sell cryptocurrency directly with others, it also lets you avoid some of the transaction fees associated with traditional exchanges. Here are three ways in which people use P2P trading to their advantage:

Arbitrage with fiat

P2P trading provides arbitrage opportunities with fiat money. With over 100 fiat currencies to choose from on Binance, for instance, you have the opportunity to benefit from the price differences between these fiat currencies.

Arbitrageurs start by calculating the price differences and potential profits before making any purchase. Below is an example of how an arbitrageur can leverage price differences.

Trading BTC/USD: If the buy price is $21,000 or €23,100 (the USD and EUR markets have different prices) and the sell price is $20,800 or €22,880, buying bitcoin and immediately selling it back in the same fiat would result in a loss of $200 or €220 (sell price - buy price).

Trading BTC/EUR: If the buy price is $21,364 or €23,500 and the sell price is $21,182 or €23,300, purchasing bitcoin with USD and selling it for EUR would lead to a profit of $182 or €200.

The above example shows how buying BTC on the US market and selling it for EUR can be more advantageous than buying and selling only on the domestic market.

Arbitrage between different exchanges

P2P trading provides plenty of opportunities for arbitrageurs, because there are often significant price differences between exchanges. Many people use P2P trading to buy and sell crypto assets in order to benefit from these differences.

They may arbitrage between different exchanges, usually through the purchase and sale of the same asset to take advantage of its price difference on different exchanges.

For example, if bitcoin sells for $21,000 on exchange A and $21,100 on exchange B, buying it on A and immediately selling it on B would result in the buyer earning $100 per bitcoin but you should consider the withdrawal and network fees.

Publish buy and sell ads

This method allows you to post an ad on a P2P trading platform, featuring the asset you are interested in buying or selling and the price at which you're willing to transact. Once your ad is posted, other platform users who see it will then decide if they want to trade with you.

If another P2P user decides to trade with you, he will send you a trade request. Once you accept the request, both parties can complete the trade. Choosing to set a higher price than the market price will ensure that you generate more revenue.

For example, you can publish an advertisement to purchase bitcoin at $20,000 and another advertisement to sell bitcoin at $20,200. This way, you can earn $200 for every 1 bitcoin that you trade.

What are the risks of Arbitrage?

While arbitrage can be beneficial to a trader, it comes with its own risks and costs. For instance, shifts in exchange rates may drive the value of a currency or asset down. In this case, a trader may experience financial loss if their asset's value decreases before they manage to sell it on another market.

In addition, there are banking fees associated with transferring assets between markets, which can eat into profits. There may also be other indirect costs, such as the cost of financing transactions and the opportunity cost of not investing funds elsewhere.

Is P2P Trading Safe?

P2P trading is generally safe but this usually also depends on the exchange and the safety measures it has in place. While older P2P exchanges came with higher risk of theft and scams, many newer P2P trading platforms have greatly improved their security measures.

A leading P2P exchange today will have an escrow service, regular security updates, and a stringent identity verification process (among other measures) to keep users safe. However, even with robust safeguards in place, all trading activity comes with risks — and P2P trading is no exception.

THE END!

www.ingramcontent.com/pod-product-compliance
Lightning Source LLC
Chambersburg PA
CBHW050726260726
48661CB00001B/90